MESSAGES
FROM SPIRIT

Also by Colette Baron-Reid

Books

Remembering the Future: *The Path to Recovering Intuition*
Your Partnership with Spirit:
Discover the Truth of Having It All (available June 2009)

Audio Programs

I Am/Grace*
Journey Through the Chakras
Magdalene's Garden*
Messages from Spirit (4-CD set and guidebook)

Card Decks

Wealth Wisdom Oracle Cards (available October 2009)
The Wisdom of Avalon Oracle Cards

*All the above are available from Hay House
except items marked with an asterisk

Please visit Hay House USA: **www.hayhouse.com**®
Hay House Australia: **www.hayhouse.com.au**
Hay House UK: **www.hayhouse.co.uk**
Hay House South Africa: **www.hayhouse.co.za**
Hay House India: **www.hayhouse.co.in**

MESSAGES FROM SPIRIT

THE EXTRAORDINARY POWER OF ORACLES, OMENS, AND SIGNS

COLETTE BARON-REID

HAY HOUSE, INC.

Carlsbad, California • New York City
London • Sydney • Johannesburg
Vancouver • Hong Kong • New Delhi

Published and distributed in the United States by: Hay House, Inc.: www.hayhouse.com • *Published and distributed in Australia by:* Hay House Australia Pty. Ltd.: www.hayhouse.com.au • *Published and distributed in the United Kingdom by:* Hay House UK, Ltd.: www.hayhouse.co.uk • *Published and distributed in the Republic of South Africa by:* Hay House SA (Pty), Ltd.: www.hayhouse.co.za • *Distributed in Canada by:* Raincoast: www.raincoast.com • *Published in India by:* Hay House Publishers India: www.hayhouse.co.in

Editorial supervision: Jill Kramer • *Design:* Tricia Breidenthal

Library of Congress Cataloging-in-Publication Data

Baron-Reid, Colette.
  Messages from spirit : the extraordinary power of oracles, omens, and signs / Colette Baron-Reid. -- 1st ed.
      p. cm.
  ISBN-13: 978-1-4019-1845-3 (tradepaper) 1. Oracles. 2. Omens. 3. Signs and symbols. I. Title.
  BF1779.B37 2008
  133.3--dc22
                                        2007047074

ISBN: 978-1-4019-1845-3

11 10 09 08   7 6 5 4
1st edition, May 2008
4th edition, July 2008

Printed in the United States of America

For Zigo and Eva

*In memory of all that
was beautiful and good*

CONTENTS

PREFACE

This book is meant to be a gift. It may seem wrapped up in strange paper and challenging string, but when you manage to cut through the ties and unfold the uneven, crinkled wrappings, there will be a treasure with profound beauty and depth, glimmering with hope and wonder.

I was given this gift, and I'm sharing it with you so that you'll know what I know—that miracles are everywhere and Spirit is whispering messages of Divine guidance and love to you whenever you're willing to listen. I wrote this book to help you remember how to enter the conversation and understand the language that Spirit has used since time began. This is a language that will send loving messages to help you on your spiritual journeys as you express Life in human form.

I come to this gift-giving place from long experience. For the past 20 years, I've made my living as an *intuitive counselor*, accessing the world of Spirit through my sixth sense in service to those who have sought me out for my Sight (my intuitive abilities), objectivity, and perspective. Because initially I was reluctant to commit to what eventually became a full-time profession, I eschewed advertising or promotion of any kind. I only had aspirations of being a musical recording artist and doggedly pursued that dream while resisting—yet accepting—doing readings to pay the bills. In spite of this, my client base grew through word of mouth to attract people from 29 countries worldwide. Although my singing career garnered me a record deal with EMI music, my work as an intuitive led me to Hay House. What began as skeptical, fearful reluctance is expressed here with an open mind, integrity, faith, and passion for what I now know to be a true calling.

I call myself an *intuitive* rather than a *psychic* in order to make the multisensory experience we all share more acceptable and hopefully more accessible. I refer to my work as an *intuitive medium* in the same way. This is because I believe that what's known as *supernatural* or *paranormal* is about the immortal consciousness we all share, accessed and translated through the sixth sense. As I've immersed myself in this world these past 20 years, researching ancient spiritual traditions, studying shamanism and psychology, reading hundreds of books, teaching, and doing readings for more than 40,000 people, what I've come to know and experience often challenges the accepted illusion of separation.

My belief is also that what we deem the *supernatural* to be is just another vastly untapped, misunderstood dimension and resource naturally available to us all. I came to this conclusion because ever since I was a child, I saw and experienced consistent evidence that time, space, and the boundaries of consciousness weren't limited in the way I was taught. Life and Death, the separation of humanity and Nature, and the concept of God being separated from us are all concepts that have been constantly challenged throughout my personal and professional experience. Although I was reluctant at first to accept that this was very real and not just a personal fluke, the repetition of the evidence has led me to conclude that there's so much more to reality than we can possibly fathom. We're more than we know, and so is the natural world.

Over the years, as I tuned my own senses to include Nature and all of Life as possible conduits for a dialogue with Divine guidance, I've seen miracles and wondrous things unfold. As I turned to Spirit for guidance and I learned to discern the messages I received, I came to believe that this force is immanent and everywhere and always willing to converse with us if we sincerely want to know the will of the Divine. All we need is to know how to read the signs and discern truth from fantasy.

This book offers you a way to explore this world through stories and interactive exercises. I hope they'll ignite the memories in your own immortal soul of a time when you knew Spirit was speaking to you from the rocks and trees, the rivers and the sea, the birds and four-legged creatures, one and all. I hope that you may come to the open acceptance that your loved ones still "live" even when they leave their bodies behind. It's my wish that this book will nudge your consciousness awake to the Unity we all reside within and to discover that Nature is another face of the Divine, longing to be in partnership with us.

Since the subject of oracles, omens, and signs as a means to access higher guidance is such a broad subject, the book is divided into three distinct parts, although they all relate to each other in some way.

Part I is dedicated to true stories that were chosen to illustrate the meaning of oracles, omens, and signs. I believe that all our life experiences are teaching tools, so I always tell my own tale, because these personal events have driven me to investigate the wonders around me. I want to have a deeper understanding of their meaning to the collective, and I share them so that you can walk a while in my shoes and see if they take you somewhere significant. My stories are all true, although I've changed some names and reconstructed some details to protect the privacy of certain individuals. Where I used real names, I've done so with written permission.

As well as being autobiographical, this book also features stories about and from some of my clients and friends. You'll meet interesting characters from my life who first introduced me to the world of Spirit and to some divinatory tools that will be explained later in these pages. You'll also be invited to explore a new perspective on the role of your animal companions and how they fit into the Divine conversation.

Part II explores the unique history of divination, methods the ancients used to ask for Divine guidance, and the origins of spiritual traditions. You'll also learn how current cultural prejudice and dismissal of oracles, omens, and signs has been influenced by old religious beliefs. Some of my views may seem a little controversial, depending on your own opinions, but my aim is to explore an ongoing dialogue rather than settle on outmoded dogma. All I ask is that you keep an open mind (then take what you like and leave the rest behind if you choose).

Part III is dedicated to illustrating how Spirit speaks to you and how you can enter the conversation. As well as plenty of stories, there are numerous modernized forms of ancient divination systems for you to explore and be amazed by. You'll also find an extensive symbol guide to aid you in understanding the symbolic language of Spirit so that you can begin to experience this extraordinary part of ordinary life, long forgotten and longing to be remembered.

In parting, I asked Spirit to send me a message today to share with you as a gift of initiation into the world I'm inviting you to explore. I got into my car and turned on the radio, and my senses amplified as chills went up my arms. Just for you, a woman's beautiful voice sang that *we are all on a journey where the wonders never cease.*

May you know how you are truly blessed.

— **Colette Baron-Reid**

INTRODUCTION

Messages from Spirit

I went to the beach today and asked for a sign about this book. The process of writing over the course of this past year has brought many answers but also many questions still to explore. That's a good thing, and representative of the true essence of looking for guidance. In fact, this is what connecting to the Divine is like. It isn't static and limited by definition, because It is always evolving just as we are.

Whether we say Spirit, the Divine, or any other name, this emergent Awareness reveals Itself to us and through us, always changing and creating something new from what was. The true miracle comes when we recognize that this Consciousness is within and inherently present everywhere. Spirit speaks to us through Nature, through each other, and through all of Life in a constant ever-flowing dialogue. The territory of oracles, omens, and signs is only one way to explore this language. It's a realm of depth and beauty and revelation.

So what does this all mean in the grand scheme of things? What is it I'm trying to convey by inviting you to explore the spiritual territory of oracles, omens, and signs? How do I create a path out of the superstition, fear, and misinterpretations that have formed walls and created fences of barbed wire and broken glass separating us from Truth? There are so many complexities, colors, shapes, and symbols in this language. How can I make all of this simple?

I say only one prayer—the only one that has ever really been answered, and answered as simply as I've asked: "Please, Spirit, help me."

As I walked by the lake today, I allowed my awareness to expand, inviting the natural world to be the vehicle for Divine guidance. The beach is like a sacred prayer path for me. It's where I find many answers in what appears to be a simple stroll by the water's edge.

Be Present

As my awareness began to focus on the walk itself, I received my first sign, which I knew was telling me to pay attention and be fully conscious in the present moment. First, let me explain. My nature is to take the same path. I start at the concrete pier near the off-leash area for the local canine citizens, where I greet the dogs by name (although I forget their owners' names most of the time). I stretch, face the east, and usually smile. I stand at the same place, say my prayer, then walk to the water and follow the beach line about a half mile to another pier, this one made from natural stones all piled up. Here, I turn around and walk back.

So why notice this? Well, there are some days when I miss everything around me. I'm thinking about other things or am having make-believe conversations in my head with people who don't know I'm working stuff out with them. Distractions aren't difficult to conjure up, even if I start out praying, "What is Your will for me today?" I still can end up thinking, *I am so freaked out that so-and-so said that!* or *I can't believe it cost that much.* In my thinking mind, sometimes I consider that I'm behind enemy lines. I miss the signs that are presented because I'm not in the moment. When I'm like that, my intuition can't connect to the *oracular consciousness*—the higher awareness in every one of us that knows the language of omens and other forms of Divine guidance.

Being present and aware is the key here. The greatest power is in the moment.

My next sign reminded me of the ever-constant emerging and evolving changes of Life. As I walked, I noticed how different things were than when I did the exact same routine the day before. Then, the beach was quiet, the waves gentle and lapping. Today, the waves were rich and powerful, pushing new seaweed fronds to the beach, depositing all kinds of goodies for the seagulls, ducks, and swans. Today, my favorite perfume, *"L'eau de Poisson,"* wafted in the breeze—and yes, that's just a fancy name for "the air smells like fish." It tells me the lake is alive. The wind doesn't always smell like that, but this day it did and I love it.

The stones I saw yesterday weren't the same ones I saw today. I noticed all these beautiful, smooth, glistening rocks that twinkled like tiddledywinks in the sand. I had never seen these before. Every step of the way was noticeably different.

Isn't that what all of Life is like? Nothing remains the same, even if we retrace our steps over and over. Everything is changing and evolving and growing. The Divine force in all things is constantly creative. All is emergent from one state to another.

This is Nature, the Divine impulse, creating itself in manifest form, an emerging, ever-revealing Consciousness writing a new story from old ones again and again. No matter how the plots change, the Infinite essence that infuses Life is Spirit. We're an integral part of this whole drama because we're made of Spirit, as is everything in the manifest world. We're also the translators of earlier stories and the ones who write new ones, many times borrowing pieces of what came before, changing them to illustrate what exists now.

I walked some more, clearly in the moment and contemplating the world around me, being part of it, immersing myself in the awareness within. Then my attention was caught by something bright white in the sand.

There, in front of me on the beach, was a huge feather lying half on the wet sand, half on the dry sand. One-third of it was pure white and fluffy like snow, and formed a wide base. Although it was lying in the dampness, the white strands were completely clean and dry, which I thought was odd. The other two-thirds of the feather was dirty brown in color and caked with dense, wet sand. It changed shade and shape from the point it emerged from the white base until it formed a twist at the end. It was as if something tangible, heavier, and completely formed came out of a fluffy, formless cloud.

The message was so clear: This is what all Life is like. The essence that allows us to fly, the fluffy white protective feathers of all of Life, is Spirit, without which there can be no flight. Yet Spirit can only soar through the bird's wing, which is both spiritual *and* material. This is true for all of us, too. We're also part of the ever-emerging consciousness of Spirit expressing itself through us.

Children of the Divine

I made myself comfortable on a rock and thought about how we find an intimate relationship with Spirit naturally. How do oracles, omens, and signs provide a bridge between the material world and its spiritual essence? I heard a voice within me say, *We are all sons and daughters of God.*

If this is true, then there must be a God—a Source—behind all our various versions of the Almighty. Trying to define the Source is like trying to put a form around something that needs to evolve and emerge through the power of its own formlessness. I believe that Source is Love; I believe that Source is Light. I believe the expression of these things is compassion.

But there are so many different ideas and myths about God and how we're supposed to relate to Him or Her. These are emergent stories, evolving as *we* evolve. They're externals, though, and if we only *compare* our externals, we will never be able to *identify* with the common impulse behind them. We'll be doomed to fight because our faith will be dependent on habits, rules, concepts, dogmas, and ideologies that represent our religion's version of God or Spirit. These will only serve to separate us if those elements are just seen myopically as memberships to exclusive clubs. Spirit doesn't rule out any methods of dialogue. It answers—no matter in what form we ask.

There's a common spirituality behind all of these external differences. Through all of our stories, we're all searching for Divine guidance. We're looking for answers, and we want them in a form that's familiar, consistent, and measurable to make us feel secure. Yet there isn't any one form that will always be the same; no single way will answer all the time. Divine dialogue is always changing and emerging as awareness within us grows. A conversation with Spirit is immersed in activity, filling itself with life and Light.

We all struggle with the same duality of ego that stands in the way of the soul: good versus evil, right versus wrong. We want the same things: We want our families to be safe, we want to survive, we want to thrive, and we want to have what's ours—whatever that may be. We want to love and be loved. We want to be happy, and we want peace of mind.

We long to know, *Who am I? What's my purpose? Why am I here? What's the meaning of Life? Who is God? Why was I born? What happens when I die? Why must I suffer, and how can I be freed from it?* And when we do receive our message from Spirit, how do we know that the guidance behind it is real? We all still need to differentiate between the voice of the soul and that of the ego. No matter how we describe the details and the steps that form the bridge, or what that bridge looks like, we still cross the same one. Essentially, we're all looking for an intimate and personal experience with the Divine.

Many of the great spiritual traditions and wisdom teachings began with the personal mystical revelation of one individual answering these questions, be it Jesus, Mohammed, Abraham, Zoroaster, Buddha, Confucius, St. Francis of Assisi, Martin Luther, St. Teresa of Avila, or any of numerous others. All are different externally in habit, form, and method, but all are essentially the same in that they address the Source.

Join the Exploration

I'm inviting you to explore what motivates all spiritual inquiry and the Source of the inquiry. And I'm calling you to look at this through the dialogue of Divine guidance bridged by oracles, omens, and signs. Infinite Spirit reveals itself to us, through us, in many ways. These methods and traditions are all legitimate ways to experience Divine guidance.

Although we'll never truly know who or what God is intellectually, we nevertheless can have a personal experience of God that is powerful and extraordinary. In this book there are many ways to achieve this intimate connection with the Divine, but these aren't the only methods. There are countless other ways and forms in which to ask the same questions that have existed since humankind first began to inquire. The ones I've included here are interesting, fun, and engaging—and best of all, they work.

Does it matter how we get there? Isn't it amazing that Spirit will give us guidance using the natural world as a medium in the dialogue? Isn't it absolutely fantastic and wonderful that we're all connected to the entirety of Life? Isn't it wonderful that we're here at all, that we're aware and conscious and able to be part of the infinite dance?

So I was amazed and humbled when I prayed, "God, help me, please," after asking for a sign, and I saw the feather as if it were placed directly on the beach for my benefit.

After all these deep thoughts and revelations that came to me on that walk, it was time to go home and write this down for you. And as I approached my car, I received another message.

A disheveled old man with matted hair and filthy clothing was leaning into the recycling box at the edge of the beach. I could smell him from a good 30 feet away. He had an odor of rotting garbage and human sweat, as if he were decaying in front of me. The stench was unbearable.

As I got closer, I could see he'd soiled himself but didn't seem to be aware of this at all. He was muttering and engrossed in taking cans out of the bin and smashing them flat with his foot. He then placed them meticulously in a pile beside him. I had to walk past him, and as I neared my car, I noticed my senses amplifying again. I knew it meant that I was to pay attention, but to what? The stinky old man?

Opening my car door, I heard him, loud as can be, yell, "Everything fits! It's all perfect! Perfect! Perfect! Perfect! Perfect! He made it that way! He did, He did!"

I got in my car and recalled a song that I hadn't thought of for years and years. It was a hymn we used to sing in my church choir when I was little:

> *All things bright and beautiful,*
> *all creatures great and small,*
> *all things wise and wonderful,*
> *the Lord God made them all.*

For a while, I sat in my car overlooking the beach and watched the man walk away, muttering to himself about how perfect the world was.

And then I looked up at the clouds that were just beginning to form ahead of me on the skyline above the water. It was perfect. Beams of light streamed through clouds that seemed like heaven's curtains being parted by the angels.

Then I noticed that the clouds were forming a huge edifice with domes and another cathedral-like structure beside it. Of course—this is what it's all about! The world is the sacred temple of the Divine. We're all made of God and Divine breath; the consciousness of God is Spirit, and it's within all of us. All of life can be used as a means of communication between the Divine and ourselves.

Spirit speaks through all of life, and this book will help show you how to join in the conversation.

So come with me and see . . .

How forever shall we all . . . blessed be.

PART I

True Encounters with Spirit

CHAPTER 1

COFFEE, TEA, AND ME

Turkish coffee was more than just a drink in my home—it was a portal to other worlds. It was a cup in which we could know the unknown, understand the past, reveal the present, and point to the future. It was also something my mother made my father promise he would never have again at a party after he let the proverbial cat out of the bag (while he was in a trance) about the secret love affairs of the neighbors. From then on, the Turkish coffee was to be drunk only on special occasions, and not be utilized as anything other than a beverage.

Still, those tiny painted cups with gold leaf at the edges and the dark, rich, thick aromatic coffee in them were swirled on our table with mysterious potential many a Sunday when I was growing up. My father remained ever curious about the patterns left by the coffee grounds caked to the insides of the cups, although he never encouraged us to learn the language of symbols that linked us and Spirit with those magical vessels. I did that on my own while failing at the law profession and other academic pursuits my parents chose for me, when I was a little older and a lot more rebellious.

Although my father spoke very little about the cups, he did say one thing when I was about ten years old that stuck with me all my life. I asked him one day why they had so much power that Mom said he couldn't look into them anymore. He said the cups and the coffee themselves had no power at all. He told me that the energy lay in the invisible relationship between the soul of the drinker and the patterns left to tell the story that the soul already knew. It was a way that the soul could speak to the thoughts of the person through symbols and images that I've come to understand as the language of Spirit.

I remember asking him why the soul had to speak to the thoughts. He replied that it was because the person's immortal soul knew everything but the mortal mind didn't. And at that point, I recall, he spent a long time philosophizing about death and immortality, which I listened to only halfheartedly because I was watching one of my escaped gerbils, Linus, wander around the back of his chair. However, I do remember listening intently to this: He said that life was all about getting those two parts of the person together so that the individual could experience peace and be aware of God. That was such a simple yet profound thing to say to a child. (Of course, it's all I think about these days.) I didn't really understand it at the time, but I sensed that all would be revealed one day as my intuition stored his words in a special place in my memory.

My mother didn't seem to like oracles back then, and my father and his coffee grounds weren't the only spirit messengers that she had to contend with in our home. Allow me to introduce Mrs. Kelly and her oracle cards. She was, besides my father, the strongest influence in my life regarding the subject of Spirit, and her wise words still echo around me today.

The Nanny Oracles

Mrs. Kelly was Scottish, and she was in her late 70s when she came into our home to be our nanny. She was an eccentric character, full of contradictions and surprises.

A psychic and a spiritualist with a penchant for horse racing, she made her way in the world by babysitting, gambling, and chatting with the deceased. (She listened to the spirits in the hopes that they'd tell her which horses to pick!) I briefly introduced her in my first book, *Remembering the Future,* but I'd like to expand on her importance in my life and my earliest introduction to the subject of oracles, omens, and signs.

I remember her vividly. She was small and slender with dark blue rheumy eyes and the crinkly white skin typical of an aged Scotswoman. I recall that she had silver white hair curled tightly around her ears, but with unruly strands that stuck out all over the place like Einstein. Her teeth, yellowed and grayed with age, were pushed together as if there wasn't enough room in her mouth. The bright pink slash of lipstick that bled into the many lines around her pursed mouth always seemed to emphasize her least attractive features. She was strange, and she fascinated me, particularly when she pulled out the deck of ordinary playing cards that she referred to as "my special oracle."

We'd sit together at the kitchen table, and Mrs. Kelly would gaze glassy-eyed at the cards spread out on the antique-lace cloth my mother had brought over to Canada from Germany. Then Mrs. Kelly would look somewhere in the air above the playing cards as if she were seeing something floating there.

Next she'd begin to ramble in her heavy Scottish brogue that at the best of times was tough to understand. But in those moments, it became even more difficult because she croaked like a frog between breaths. What I heard sounded like snippets of prayer, so I'd sit quietly, making sure I didn't fidget. I didn't dare interrupt a conversation with God, even though I was looking forward to tea and "biscuits" (cookies) afterward. Continuing to gaze from her cards to a mysterious unseen place just above them, she'd find her pace after a while. I traced the patterns in the lace while I listened intently as she told me things that wouldn't make sense for another 30 to 40 years. Even though I was only five when this first occurred, I vividly remember the gifts she left me with.

Using her playing cards as an oracle tool, Mrs. Kelly did what most adults never had—she distracted me from the cookies she'd promised to give me. Instead, I was captivated by the way her eyes changed, as if they were looking inward and far, far away at the same time. I was mesmerized by the physical shift as well: Her features softened as if the very bones underneath them took on another, more beautiful, shape. Her blue-veined hands, normally twisted and bent with arthritis, had a youthful suppleness when she effortlessly shuffled the cards. What I know now—which eluded my five-year-old sensibilities—is that I was witnessing Spirit alter the features of an old woman as she expressed her intuitive vision.

When Mrs. Kelly read her cards, I felt the room become active with another kind of energy. My senses were focused and amplified as I heard her speak my story. It made no sense to me at the time, but I knew that every word was important. It was as if I were hearing it through "different" ears. I didn't know I was experiencing her words through *clairaudience,* an amplified sense of hearing that occurs when receiving messages from Spirit. I didn't know intellectually or consciously that there was a higher meaning. I *did* understand that I was experiencing something very old within myself—older and wiser than what I was at the time. It was truly another kind of knowing; the awareness of Spirit within me was listening.

Long before I was aware of my own intuitive blessings, I was fortunate to have experienced wisdom from Spirit relayed to me through this truly gifted woman. Her prophecies for me, spoken on many different occasions, took years to unfold and only came to mind when they manifested. But each time they did, that same "older awareness" would seem to come awake and speak to me. When something happened, I'd say to myself, *Holy moly—Mrs. Kelly told me that. Wow!* And sometimes I even heard her voice in some distant place in my mind. (Imagine a really old Scottish lady with a heavy accent when you read the following words.)

- "You have the Sight."

- "There's music all around you."

- "You'll be on stages all over the world."

- "You're meant to help many people in a very unusual way."

- "Don't ever forget that what makes you different is a blessing."

- "You have a special kinship with animals, and they with you."

- "You will love life, and life will love you back."

These statements meant nothing to me when I first heard them. Imagine my young brain trying to wrap itself around the phrase "meant to help people in an unusual way." At that age, that meant helping somebody pick up worms off the playground after it rained—that was it, worm picking. And as for the talk of "music," I did love it, but I didn't know what a "stage" was. On the other hand, I was learning to bang a xylophone before nap time at kindergarten. That must have been what she meant.

Kinship was a strange word, which is why I remembered it, although I believed it had something to do with a special boat. I did understand that I loved animals, because I was surrounded by them. Our golden retriever Rascal had a litter of puppies, and we had a budgie named Schnookyputz. Then there was our guinea pig (whose name I forget), who hung out in one of my mom's apron pockets. Mickey the mouse got to ride in the other one. And there were all the other cool friends in the garden, some of whom my mother insisted were imaginary. So when Mrs. Kelly spoke of my life, that fresh five-year-old point of view was pretty limited. Yet she saw these things, all of which have transpired in my adult life.

Mother

My mother begrudgingly allowed Mrs. Kelly to use our house to read the oracle cards for visitors while she (my mom) was out with my father. She tolerated Mrs. Kelly's "tea parties" because our nanny was a strict disciplinarian and made family life easy. Truth be known, although she'd never admit it then, my mother liked getting her cards read, too. She loved it, but she didn't want her own family members communicating with Spirit.

I know my mother was deeply conflicted about my intuitive gifts. I had recurring nightmares from the age of three until I was about five that were permeated with details of real events of my mother's life before she came to Canada, long before I was born. My dreams intruded upon her hard-won safety and new identity. (I spoke at length about this in my first book, *Remembering the Future*.) My mother hid the fact that she was the daughter of a Jew killed in Dachau and that she'd experienced the atrocities of war in Berlin. How could I—a small child living in the safety of the New World and raised as a Christian, never knowing anything about war or my mother's ties to the Holocaust—dream about these true and intimate details? My mother wanted to protect me from others and from myself . . . and she wanted to shield herself from me. She had too many secrets to keep from her little girl's invasive Sight.

She considered Mrs. Kelly's cards only slightly acceptable as they, too, had the power to speak about the past and uncover secrets my mother wanted to forget. Safety and security in the present and in the future were acceptable topics for the cards to reveal. The past was forbidden.

Life with Mrs. Kelly

Mrs. Kelly was sometimes difficult to understand, too. She had rules, and boy, were they ever followed. I went to bed on time and always ate my dinner right down to the roses on the china plate, even if I hated the yucky shepherd's pie on it. On the other hand, she reassured me that the fairies in the garden weren't just my imagination, and she encouraged my young mind to embrace such mysteries. But then she'd turn around and instill her strict discipline. In her own way, Mrs. Kelly was setting up valuable lessons for me regarding the oracular path. There's no excuse for breaking rules in the spirit world.

But she, too, was only human. As I mentioned, she loved to gamble and was convinced that talking to the dead helped her pick winners. She didn't win a lot, so I'm not quite sure how she got around that rather glaring fact. She was hard of hearing, though, so perhaps that was the main reason. "Oh my goodness, the spirits said 'Vanilla Bean' not 'Manila's Dream'!" Regardless, win or lose, she loved to bet on the horses as much as she loved to read cards for anyone who needed guidance or who was indulging a forbidden curiosity after church.

Sometimes when my parents were visiting friends on Sundays, I had to go to church with Mrs. Kelly. That was fine because I loved it. There she'd be, huddled together with a couple of other old ladies with violet and blue hair, wearing big funny hats and white gloves in solemn and pious solidarity. Then she'd invite them to come to our house, and that's when the party started—a tea party, yes, but complete with all sorts of Sunday "spirits." The ladies would sit around the kitchen table all atwitter, until Mrs. Kelly croaked a few times like a frog. Poor thing, she couldn't help it, but it did give her an air of strange, mysterious authority. She shooed me away, but I always sneaked a peek from behind the door.

She consulted her playing cards and dispensed her timely and important vision to her friends, and of course the racing form would be part of this ritual. Anyway, after an hour of hushed tones and knowing glances, their moods would levitate to a loud chatter, and it would be time for a real cup of tea. That's when I usually heard my name uttered in a harsh-toned, high-pitched, heavy Scottish brogue. I knew she'd discovered that the cookies were missing. Try as I might to convince her, Mrs. Kelly didn't buy that "the spirits came and ate them all." *Oops!* In retrospect, I think I should have blamed the fairies in the garden.

I loved Mrs. Kelly, but when I look back now, I realize that I didn't know her very well at all. But I knew she had a strong impact on my life. The times when she acted as an *oracle messenger* on my behalf were distinct and ultimately unforgettable, even if time caused them to fade slightly into some "in-between places" in my mind. Only recently have I begun to recount these episodes to myself as I trace the steps of my experiences with Spirit.

Close Enough Doesn't Count

Eventually, my parents' need for Mrs. Kelly's services came to an end. But that didn't mean that our special bond ceased. She read her cards for me many times over the years, long after she left our employ. The last one I remember was when I was 14 and getting ready to leave for Europe with my parents for the summer. She described my husband, complete with all the details surrounding the union.

Mrs. Kelly said his family was from a Germanic language–speaking country, but they lived somewhere exotic. She stated that his voice would tell me that he was the one and that he had piercing blue green eyes that were like a clear ocean. She even told me he was in a rock band, which I thought was extremely cool. I expected to meet this man by the time I was 18, settle down, and live happily ever after. She forgot to mention that I wouldn't encounter him until I was 44 years old. Or maybe she did, and my mind blanked that part out. After all, she was talking marriage! To a rock star! With great eyes!

And this is what I dreamed up from that: He was just around the next corner. I would have six fabulous kids and three cars and lots of money. Then I would be a rock star, too, and have even more children and more money and live happily ever after somewhere in another galaxy where my parents couldn't visit. Of course, she actually said none of that, but I had a great imagination. This shows how important it is to discern what you're hearing during any oracle reading. I think I was doing more dreaming than listening.

In fact, that summer I did have my first real teenage romance with a young Norwegian boy. He and his family came to the resort town where my family was staying on the rocky Croatian coast in the former Yugoslavia. I remember him vividly. He had soft blue eyes and hair the color of early wheat. His skin was tanned a beautiful dark brown, in contrast to his Scandinavian blondness. Bottom line: He was the cutest boy ever!

We held hands and exchanged innocent kisses. I was terribly shy (who knew?), as was he. He spoke very little English, and I spoke no Norwegian, but I learned he was in a rock band in Oslo that met in his parents' garage. He wanted me to join him there the following year.

Now not all of these details fit perfectly with Nanny's oracle message, but they came pretty close. Norway was an exotic place to me, and his accent sounded Germanic. Although I didn't see any green in his blue eyes, the fact that he had blond hair and sang in a rock band was enough for me. *Yippee!* Plus, Norway was far away from my parents. I did what I know many of us do: I fit the oracle message into a size and shape that suited my desire.

Back then, my adolescent mind could only see a few years at a time, so I was certain that my Norwegian sweetheart was "The One." We wrote to each other for a few months, declaring undying love; but then distance won out, and we forgot each other all too easily as our lives unfolded on opposite sides of the ocean. So much for love in the cards.

When we met, I was convinced that Mrs. Kelly had predicted he would be my husband. So many of the things she said sounded like him. But there was no "Aha!" feeling, nor were any of my ordinary senses amplified through my sixth sense. I intellectualized our meeting instead of feeling it with the familiarity of inner wisdom imparted by a higher consciousness. (This is one of the things you'll learn about in this book.)

Of course that boy wasn't "The One." And in my young mind that was the greatest tragedy ever.

An Oracle Is Better Late Than Never

My true experience of that oracle happened exactly 30 years later. I met my husband, Marc, via the Internet and heard his warm and friendly voice on the phone before meeting him in person. I knew instantly that *he* was "The One." Hearing his voice took me intuitively to the friendliest inner sense of awareness; it was like coming home to a place I'd always wanted to go to but hadn't been to yet within myself. I'd never had that first reaction when meeting anyone. I was really excited and calm at the same time. *Oh boy,* I thought, *here we go.*

On our first date, Marc told me some interesting things that brought me back to the heightened sensitivity I'd had when I first heard about my destiny from Mrs. Kelly. I could sense her presence when he began to talk about himself.

Marc had been in a famous-for-a-minute Canadian rock band for a few years. That really got my attention since I was familiar with the group and knew all the words to their first radio hit when they were popular in the late '80s. His father was Dutch-born (that rang the Germanic-language bell), but he had been brought up in Indonesia. His family had also lived in Pakistan for a couple of years when Marc was little. Okay, those places were definitely pretty exotic. He also happened to have the most amazing piercing greenish blue eyes and hair the color of dark wheat that bleached blond in the summer. Bottom line, he was drop-dead gorgeous on top of everything, and I could barely breathe when we met in a Starbucks for the first time.

One morning, exactly a month to the day after our first meeting, Marc asked me to read for him. I love oracle cards and have a shelf full of all kinds, so that day I took down my favorite tarot deck—*Universal Waite.* I was concerned that I might spook him if I just used my gift alone. Cards or other objects at least appear to be the ones delivering the message. I think sometimes people are more comfortable asking what I see in the cards than acknowledging that I can read with nothing but the air surrounding me. Regardless, tools do work, and they're fun to use to talk with Spirit.

So Marc shuffled the cards and chose 21. They presented an undeniable message that I couldn't reveal to him. Basically, the reading said we would be with each other, own property, work together, fall in love, get married, travel the world, and live with happiness and spiritual growth. *Yikes. Oh my God!*

How was I going to tell him this? We'd only been dating for a month, and both of us declared that we weren't ever getting married again (we'd both had unsuccessful previous marriages). I think I was lying to myself about that, but he meant it. He was clear from the beginning that he wasn't staying in Toronto. He'd lived in Los Angeles for a few years and was determined to move back there to pursue a career as a screenwriter. That day he was asking about his success in that endeavor.

I chose not to tell him what I saw because I felt the message would have spooked him. So instead, I said he would do really well in life, no worries, all was well, and I didn't think the cards felt like giving details that morning. I honestly believe that Spirit gave me a glimpse of the future to revisit during those times when my feminine insecurities inevitably got the better of me. While I put the cards away, I noted how all my senses had amplified into another knowing. I allowed my consciousness to wrap itself around the message and store it in a safe place before asking, "Now can we go for breakfast?"

I waited six months for Marc to figure out how sure he was about us as a couple. Talk about having to learn patience! Knowing that the oracle was a test in faith, those six months were excruciating. I felt like a kid again, obsessively picking daisy petals: He loves me; he loves me not; he has to love me; no, he doesn't; he is The One; he may be The One; please let him be The One; *ad nauseam.* So much for the "let go and let God" concept. This is an obvious example of getting attached to the message and an outcome that has yet to unfold. After all, staring at a kettle won't make the water boil any faster.

In the end, I learned the most powerful lesson, which is that I had to merge intuition with faith and surrender to whatever Spirit wanted me to discover and to do. I learned to accept someone exactly as he was and to keep surrendering to his right to choose. Also, I learned to let go of my ego desire and self-centered fear. Needless to say, Marc didn't move to Los Angeles. I pulled the right daisy petal: He loved me.

Ours is truly the deepest love. I've never even liked a man as much as I like him. I admire and respect him, and we never say disrespectful words to each other. He inspires me and makes me laugh. When we got married, we said divorce would never be an option. Home is where we are—anywhere we are—as long as we're together. Mrs. Kelly was right, even though it happened 30 years later than I expected. It was worth waiting for.

Predictions, Probable Futures, and the Power of Now

Now here's an important point about predictions: They're all based and seen in the now. It's like being able to see how many seeds are planted in the ground and knowing whether killer worms on their way from China will eat the sprouts by such and such a date, or whether the soil will become richer and the seeds will grow and flourish in an explosion of fabulousness. That said, knowing an outcome doesn't ensure the security of the steps you need to take to get there. Things can change. You still need to live the experiences directly in front of you on the path to your destination, which is how you get there anyway. True soul work is always done in the present.

Predictions are but markers on the journey pointing to those things potentially placed by Fate. But you only find out whether they were right when you actually arrive. Divine guidance is about how to choose the next right action along the path, with each moment being a step to the destination. Still, we receive these markers for a reason, and knowing what they are can play an important role in self-discovery.

Going My Way

Actually, only a few years ago (before I met Marc), I traded readings with a well-respected Toronto psychic named Kim White. She was no Mrs. Kelly. Kim, a beautiful woman in her 40s, was still as stunning as when she was a fashion model in Paris some 20 years ago. She was deeply spiritual with unerring integrity. Although we approached our work very differently, her fresh and honest perspective was exactly what I needed. I don't get more than one reading a year for reasons I'll discuss later, and I decided I'd allow myself to be "witnessed" by Kim. I was in transition and wanted to see what Spirit had in store for me. I had some pretty specific agendas, though, and my ego was having a heyday masquerading as my soul.

Kim used oracle cards and prayed for guidance before she began. She started by telling me some very accurate facts about my past, which I believe always establishes credibility. Then she asked, "Who is Marc?" I immediately got all excited because I liked someone named Michael. I agreed that the letter *M* was correct, but not the name. She insisted it was Marc, not Michael, but eventually capitulated to my inflexible and arrogant argument. Then she proceeded to tell me all the qualities that this man had, which were similar to the person I was interested in, but not quite right. Boy oh boy, was I determined that Michael was The One, and what she said was close enough. Needless to say, the romance with him wasn't meant to be, no matter how badly I wanted the predictions to fit the bill. I refused to listen to my own intuition, which was trying desperately to be heard over the din of my wants, which were shouting the lyrics to the song "My Way."

After finally surrendering to Spirit's guidance, I learned some extremely important life lessons and got a chance to look deeply at some of the wounds I hadn't yet mended. So in fact, the oracle reading was a catalyst for painful but necessary reflection and healing.

I let it all go, turning it over to Spirit with detachment. Then, a year after my ego grabbed the reading and made it what I wanted it to be instead of what Spirit had in mind, Marc entered the picture—exactly as Kim had said he would. Mrs. Kelly and Kim White saw identical things some 40 years apart. What was most important about all of this wasn't the romantic aspect, but the lessons of spiritual and personal growth that Marc and I have come together to explore.

It's so easy to get lost in the form the lessons take, instead of looking to the higher meanings and the greater depths they invite us to experience. Mrs. Kelly told me this many times, but I was too immature to understand the greater wisdom imparted through the doorways opened by her cards. Then when I was mature, even with all my knowledge, I still got caught in the desire for an outcome that was to elude me.

Over the years, as each experience that she foresaw appeared as a necessary lesson, I remembered what I couldn't understand when I first heard it. Yet I always remember the intuitive feelings I had at the time. This is how all of us experience oracles. They continue to unfold within us long after their message is planted in our awareness.

Mrs. Kelly was given "access" to my story, and my memory of her has given me great comfort when I needed it most. In the darkest moments of my life, I remembered the sound of her heavy Scottish brogue deepening as she gazed at the cards and then away. I didn't know she was talking to me about my life to come . . . I thought she was practicing a sad poem:

- "You'll think you'll be defeated, but you will triumph."

- "You'll enter dark places, but angels will be there."

- "You'll never lose the Light."

- "Beware the drink. Sadness. So much sadness."

- "A river of tears will flow to wash you clean and pure."

- "All will be well."

- "Jesus loves you."

- "God loves you."

Whenever I found myself at the end of another failed love affair, I'd suddenly remember snippets of other things that had sounded so foreign to me as a child:

- "Many men will love you but not love you."

- "You will be happy later, but patience will be very hard."

- "You will find the truest love."

- "Patience, little one."

- "Patience . . ."

When I began my career as an intuitive, I remembered clearly the words of the secret conversation between Mrs. Kelly and my mother that I overheard while listening from behind the dining-room door. "Your little one has the Sight," said Mrs. Kelly. "You know she does . . . she does."

And my mother said, "Shh, be quiet. We don't need this. It's just her imagination. She has a big, wild imagination."

Nevertheless, Mrs. Kelly told me, "You have the Sight. You have the Sight, but it will be many years before you can truly see." *Cool, I won't need glasses like everybody else in my family,* I thought. Such was the no-nonsense mind of a nosy, eavesdropping child.

All of this made sense bit by bit over the years. I wrote at length in my first book, *Remembering the Future,* about my early life as I struggled with addiction and alcoholism, the aftermath of gang rape, the burden of my intuitive abilities, the broken dreams of my career as a singer, and many failed relationships. Then came the blessings of surrender and spiritual awakening, followed by the grace of continuous sobriety, a successful return to music, my work as an intuitive counselor, and every step that led me here—including meeting Marc and coming to Hay House. But this book isn't meant to be about all that. It's about how this was all foreseen through signs and omens and oracle messages years before. All those years ago, Mrs. Kelly had been given a map by Spirit to show to me.

Spirit Sends a Map

I realize now that even as a five-year-old without the understanding that comes with maturity, I took the special map that Mrs. Kelly gave me and stored it somewhere safe in my soul. When I needed to find my way, the map was unrolled by an invisible hand. My soul released it back to me each time I neared a point in my destiny. I was transformed by the memory as more was revealed one day at a time. It's the same for everyone. Long after a message is received, stored away, and assumed forgotten, the soul can unroll the map a little at a time (and for some, it's revealed all at once).

For a few years, I actually called my work *spiritual cartography* when I insisted on being referred to as something other than a *psychic*. The problem was that nobody seemed to know that *cartography* meant the art of mapmaking, so I changed my designation to *intuitive counselor*. Still, I frequently refer to the path of each individual's journey as a sacred map of potentiality, where destiny and fate could meet with free will and choice. It's just like an astrological map, where there's a keen sense of seeing events and looking at where a person should be staying on the charted path.

One of my dearest friends reminded me of this the other day when we were talking about how far I'd come. She told me that the map metaphor was the most accurate description she'd heard of her reading with me. She said it had been like unfolding the magical map of her life.

Mrs. Kelly planted some important ideas in my mind that grew deep roots and became the strongest foundations for the beliefs I have today. She told me that there were other dimensions of reality that surround all of us. As humanity evolved and expanded its influence over the natural world, much of that was forgotten, and we began to rely more and more on our intellects. I remember sitting with Mrs. Kelly in the garden when I was in my teens (she was well into her late 80s then). She said wistfully that when we lost our understanding of custodianship and began to look at the world as a place to dominate so that it would serve only our needs, Spirit began to fade away into the mists. She also kept referring to the future as a map with invisible markers where our destiny and fate could be discovered.

For me, it's like rolling out that map and seeing things magically appear on it, sometimes only after I've reached a destination. What may have been invisible at the time is clear in hindsight. I realized that the times when I thought I was most alone and deeply suffering were actually when angels had appeared on my path, but I had never seen them in advance.

I've Seen What I Believe

I've never been able to coerce a meeting with beings like angels, but they tease me once in a while with an appearance. Fairies, angels, and other such creatures exist all over the world; and many ordinary people frequently see and experience them. It's truly a case of "believe it when you see it." I've seen, which is why I believe. But my experience doesn't have to be believed or duplicated by anyone. My beliefs have evolved and my awareness has grown as I've matured. The path to know Spirit and receive Divine guidance is an individual one, and if I needed such things to get my attention, so be it. Your experience may be different, but always remember that it's equally valid. All paths lead to the Light if you're willing to illuminate the shadows.

Mrs. Kelly gave me the greatest gift, although I didn't know it—nor did I implement it for some time. She taught me to respect myself and to honor the life I was given and all that it entailed. It would be many years before I could do so. Today, I know that a strong spirit is essential to withstand the scorn of others. My soul can never be defeated by an outside threat of abandonment. The Light will never abandon me as long as this knowledge—not my ego—is the source of my being in the world. I know I'm not the judge of others.

Mrs. Kelly told me that Spirit was speaking to her through the cards and that an oracle was someone who spoke that message to help give guidance or shed light on a person's path. She told me that time and space were illusions. I know Spirit is everywhere in Nature and in me, as she said. She also agreed with me when I pointed out the halos around the stained-glass images of the saints and angels and said I thought it meant that all life is holy. In one of her oracle readings she said that I would know that as fact one day, but I had no clue what she meant. I do now. Mrs. Kelly's oracle message continues to unfold even as I write this book.

※§※

I don't remember the exact day when I heard that Mrs. Kelly had died, but I do remember smelling her sweet and musty lavender-scented talcum powder, tinged with a bitter note of halitosis (she had the worst breath), for days before I was told the news. And I'd smell those odors once in a while for a couple of years afterward. It's one of the first memories I have of one of my five senses alerting me to the spirit of someone who has passed over. I remember feeling that Mrs. Kelly would remain near me somehow . . . and I honestly think she has.

So when I look at my own oracle cards, some days I wonder if she's there, hovering around me and whispering messages in my ear. I've also wondered if my dad has been present when I've looked into the oracle messages hidden around the edges of the many cups of Turkish coffee that have passed in front of me over the last 20 years.

※§※

So where did this immersion in the world of oracles lead me? How about to the dentist? (You weren't expecting that, were you?)

DELPHI AT
THE DENTIST

This past year it became obvious to me that I couldn't avoid the dentist any longer, and I decided to get all the work done that I'd been told I needed about eight years ago. I mean, what if I were standing in front of an audience, toothless? Nope, that just wouldn't do—and trust me, I was heading that way, all because I was terrified to be restrained. Sure, I wouldn't be held down by the hygienist, but I'd be unable to move unless I wanted a metal instrument accidentally stuck up my nose. I've hated going to the dentist since I was little, anyway. I've tried everything over the years, from hypnotherapy to affirmations, core-belief reengineering to acupuncture, but nothing could alleviate my worsening hysteria about the drills, the chair, the noise, and the looming figure of a man with his hands in my mouth. I'm even breaking into a sweat right now as I write about it.

So off I went to the best professional in Toronto who specialized in dental work . . . asleep. What? A sleeping dentist? Dentistry Edgar Cayce–style—you know, the sleeping prophet? (Never mind; I thought it was funny.) No, really. The patient sleeps, gets fabulous new teeth, and spends a fortune.

The first couple of times I went, I was in no way upset by the experience. My fabulous dentist insisted on educating me about every little detail of my oral-surgery nightmare. The problem was that I had no interest in such knowledge and just thinking about it gave me anxiety. I know that he believed it would be reassuring, but I had to recite nursery rhymes in my head to block out his voice while smiling at his handsome face, appreciating his extraordinary intelligence, and admiring his eloquent hand gestures.

Mary had a little lamb. . . . Just let me go to sleep and tell me you fixed the problem, I thought. *Her fleece was . . .*

Then there was the appointment where I didn't need to go under completely, and the staff offered me something to just calm my nerves, which is a common solution, especially for a patient like me. They offered me the gas—nitrous, I believe it's called.

So after much research and reassurance from other longtime clean-and-sober acquaintances that this wouldn't lead me back into my past problems, I agreed to get the gas. I'd had it in an emergency dental situation years before but had no memory of it. I'm pretty sure that's the main reason why it doesn't seem to trigger people with addiction histories, as it has no recall effect. So I decided to do it.

Now before I get into the fun that ensued, I need to digress for just a minute.

Operating on Fumes

When I decided to write this book, I set out to trace the history of oracles to find out more about others who have acted as messengers in their times and what it was like for them. One of the most interesting things I discovered was a little something about the oracle at Delphi. The priestesses who served in the Temple of Apollo, dispensing wisdom from Spirit to the Greeks in a well-respected tradition that lasted 1,400 years, had a secret. They got themselves a little inebriated. Whether they knew it or not, perched on their three-legged stools, they got stoned.

Although there's still some argument and controversy about all this, many archaeologists have concluded that there was a definite fissure on the side of the mountain where the temple was built. This gap emitted a mixture of mind-altering gases. The structure was directly above it, and the intoxicating fumes came up from the ground right into the priestess's chamber.

So when someone says that "the ethers" spoke through a priestess to deliver an oracle message, it's really true. Although back then, *ether* was the name for the unseen intelligence of Divine Spirit. The actual gas that we call ether today floats up from the ground and inebriates anyone who breathes the fumes.

This upset me at first, as my capacity to use my sixth sense on behalf of others has only been undistorted in sobriety. When I was young and struggled with my addictions, I can honestly say that when partaking in drugs, my intuition gave me no such oracular wisdom. Or if I did receive it, I was too messed up to understand it or put it to good use.

Then again, my recurring dreams of being surrounded by fumes in an ancient temple finally made sense. And looking back, I remember some isolated moments of extraordinary clarity that did make me wonder. Obviously, however, there's a gigantic chasm of difference separating recreational drug use and sacred ritual. I hadn't been spending my time sitting in a temple as a priestess, channeling messages from Apollo while getting high on some kind of natural gas, now had I?

There are, in fact, many spiritual traditions that include the use of psychotropic and hallucinogenic plants as a means to source wisdom from Spirit. Many such ancient practices still exist in various cultures, predominantly in South America, Mexico, and Africa. There are also sacred-plant traditions in the native cultures of Australia and North America.

Indigenous peoples have used peyote, psychedelic mushrooms, and other vision-inducing plants as a means of connecting to non-ordinary states of consciousness in shamanic rituals for healing for thousands of years. These conduits are also used in order to seek wisdom from the world inhabited by spirit forms that are considered as real as beings in the physical, waking world. They induce the same experience as the gas that supposedly launched the Delphic oracles into alternate realities to retrieve messages for their seekers.

It's interesting to note that the use of these substances serves an important purpose. They enable the messengers to release their tight hold on personal identity and their perception of the physical world, in order to shift more easily to a state of consciousness in tune with Spirit. This is crucial to opening up to a higher or non-ordinary awareness, and you can get there in many ways that don't include the use of mind-altering substances.

These sacred traditions have been around for a long, long time. However, similar states of non-ordinary awareness can also be accessed through drumming rituals and ecstatic dance and, of course, meditation. I'm going to stick to those avenues. I've been clean and sober for 22 years at the time of this writing (and I plan to stay that way), so I leave wacky plants, drugs, alcohol, or sacred gas for those capable of imbibing.

There's just one exception: the dentist. And that brings me back to my story.

What a Gasbag!

The gas the dentist used had a very interesting property: It completely opened up my capacity to pick up information about whoever was in the room, unless I consciously worked hard to think about something else. It was, for me, an invitation to watch a new personal TV show called *All in the Dental Assistant's Family.*

The first time I experienced this effect, I began garbling happily through the gas mask, relaying intimate details about this poor unsuspecting girl's boyfriend and his colorful family. Let's just say that I was in the chair way past the scheduled length of my appointment. Between the necessary metal clanking in my mouth and my spitting out a free reading, the hygienist and I were in the room for so long that she got yelled at. I bet the laughter was a dead giveaway that something unusual was going on.

This happened a couple more times, and I began to compare the dental gas with the unique oracular properties of the fumes at Delphi. No wonder those ancient Greeks could do what they did—give them some gas and let them babble away. However, it would only work undistorted if the priestess was truly psychologically balanced and spiritually clear, as well as psychic.

I can just imagine the information that could have been imparted to the leader of an army who was wondering if pillaging a neighboring country would be worth the loss of life. Coming as an oracle message from a priestess who was an average girl with unresolved emotional issues and stoned on hallucinogenic gas, he might have heard: "Sure, go ahead—rape and pillage and blow their houses down! It will be fun, and a great nation will fall."

Reassured and confident, off he'd go to face the worst defeat of his life while watching *his* great nation fall. Oops. That actually happened and is a very famous Delphic boo-boo. Now we may know why.

I wasn't sure I was going to include all theses stories in this book, but something happened while I was mulling over whether or not to share my experiences at the dentist. I had to go back.

This time I got another hygienist, Bessie—new to me—and I decided that I'd control my mind through a specific meditation. Nothing could make me give another intrusive reading at the dentist—not this time. I'd start fresh.

The appointment went smoothly. I managed to spend the entire experience on a sandy beach, frolicking with dolphins in the sea of my mind. Whew! I was safe, she was safe, and all was well.

The work wasn't finished, however, and I was told that I had to come back. It takes forever to get an appointment there, so I expected to wait a couple of months.

Then the receptionist asked, "Can you come tomorrow at 11? Bessie just got a cancellation."

It turned out that I, too, had a cancellation, so I said yes.

In the chair again the next day, I relaxed and began to conjure up images of my dolphin friends. The problem was that they wouldn't stay in my mind. The minute I made the dolphin connection, it was as if an invisible force was changing channels on my meditation remote control! Instead, I began to see other images intrude upon my lovely beach scene.

My inability to meditate was definitely a sign, a clear indication that I was meant to be relaying an oracle message to Bessie. I kept seeing her talking about getting pregnant, being pregnant, upset that she wasn't pregnant, trying anyway, *ad infinitum*. The only way to get rid of these visions was to say something.

Great, I thought. *Here we go again. The oracle has arrived at the dentist.*

So I told Bessie what I knew, and she confirmed that this was indeed happening. I then launched into all the intimate details of her past relationship; her new marriage; and the important psychological ramifications of her experience, karma, and meaning of life.

Bring on the gas, never mind cleaning the teeth.

I tell this story because of its impact on both Bessie and me. Sure, the other times the gas elicited such information, I knew something was going on—but this book wasn't on my mind then. I wasn't looking at the impact of receiving an oracle message, omen, or sign.

This time was different. All of a sudden, the air around me became foggy. I heard the name Michael, related to her husband, and I knew that this Michael was deceased. She confirmed that he was her husband's father. I could hear his voice, but then I received an image of a stocky, well-built Greek man who seemed to be in front of a welding tool and electric wires. I heard that his name was Nick.

Do I tell her? I wondered.

More teeth cleaning happens.

I told her.

She confirmed that Nick was her father, who was an electrician, and I said, "He passed in your early 30s."

She answered, "Yes."

Then I saw a picture of Jesus and a coffin. I assumed this meant that her father had died at Easter, as it was coming up, and it would make sense that the anniversary of the passing would be soon.

The Jesus part was right, but Easter was wrong. She told me that he had passed at Christmas.

Stunned, the poor girl continued with my teeth, while I drifted around in another dimension, wondering what would happen next. And where were my dolphins?

I made a mental note to ask psychic medium John Holland about this. I felt set up in a weird way, like I couldn't leave until I'd done what I was supposed to. I also felt that I was a part of something meaningful for Bessie, and I surrendered to whatever this synchronicity required of me.

Then I heard the name Peter—no, Patti—or Panni?

"Does this make sense?" I asked.

She told me that her mother's name was Panniotta. Then an amazing thing happened (not that all of this wasn't pretty wild). I heard a man's voice say, "Tell your mother you're the result of my love for her in June."

I relayed the message, and Bessie looked confused, but then I saw another image, like a birthday cake. I asked, "When is your birthday?"

"Today."

Together, we counted backward to June—nine months.

Happy Birthday, Bessie.

I really wonder sometimes if the people on the other side can spot those of us with the receptive capacity to hear them and then orchestrate these events. I wonder, *Does it take much planning? Are we like special wandering phone booths? Do we have a certain glow so that they can see us and tell where we may be going? Did Bessie's deceased father and father-in-law set it up so that somebody cancelled his appointment—just to line me up with some gas so they could make a call to reach out and say "Happy Birthday"?* Who knows for sure? It's entertaining to imagine, as no one has really shown me exactly how it all works. I just know that it does.

When it comes to receiving information from those who have passed over, I've gotten over my deep attachment to my skepticism. I resisted this experience for years mostly because I couldn't explain it, but that's no longer the case. I accept that these things are very real, they happen to me frequently on tour when I'm giving readings in front of large audiences, and the information can be confirmed.

The impact of delivering such an intimate message to someone I don't know is most important. To see myself used by Spirit in such a way—as a conduit for someone else's wonder and peace of mind—is an extraordinary gift. I am humbled by it daily. Seeing someone's face light up in awe after receiving the information is incredible.

However, to actually tune in to those trying to communicate is a strange feeling for me. It's like I'm only a receiver and translator for incoming images, symbols, names, and words that I must relay to someone else. There are feelings, too. I'm privy to a sense of love that's transformative and healing, which passes between both sides. I'm careful not to intrude with my opinions, and I'm very aware that this isn't about me.

I left the dentist's office, an oracle messenger no more, having done my job in passing an important message of love from a father in heaven to his daughter on Earth. Both of us were reminded of the extraordinary power of Spirit during that spontaneous session. Bessie received the most unusual birthday present of her life, and I now have the cleanest teeth on the planet.

More Tales from the Other Side

I was willing to go through all that dentistry because I'd been invited on the Sylvia Browne/Hay House tour, which was to take place on a cruise ship, and I didn't want any teeth issues to screw it up. God forbid I'd need an emergency root canal while delivering a message to someone out at sea.

When I had my meeting with Reid Tracy, the president of Hay House, about the cruise, I expressed to him that I was fearful about becoming so public with my work—especially in light of the kind of work I do. People came to me only by word of mouth, so I never really had to define my services or put them in any particular category. I was comfortable in claiming the name *intuitive* rather than *psychic,* which I felt covered all the bases in communicating with Spirit.

"I don't talk to dead people," I said in the meeting. "Well, I do, but I can't be 100 percent certain that I do, so we have to leave that out."

"Don't worry," Reid assured me. "We have enough people who do that."

Phew.

Why was it so important for me to define what I *didn't* do? Up until the point I found myself at Hay House, I knew something was going on with me regarding this subject, but I was skeptical about whether it was real—talking to the dead, that is. I always knew that the information I was receiving was *very* real.

I understand that it's important for me to be confident that what I'm doing is legitimate, but frankly, until recently I had a very difficult time accepting that I was truly talking to the dead. It's important, however, that I don't deceive myself about the source of information. It's only over this past year that I've become a true believer, although I'm vigilant about the manner in which I receive the messages. Is this a communication from *Spirit* or from *a spirit*? Similar impact—*mucho* big difference.

The Beginning of Believing

Ever since I began doing readings, I've found that every so often I spontaneously receive information about a deceased person during someone's session. Names, events, descriptions of objects, or illnesses leading up to their deaths would be provided once in a while. My clients were mostly convinced that I was communicating with those who had passed on. Sometimes I thought so, too—but mostly I was convinced that I was just picking up data from the past through the intuitive faculty called *retrocognition,* the term for knowing the past without prior information about it.

Retrocognition is how I anchor my vision when I read for people. I allow my awareness to view someone's past and find threads and patterns leading up to the present that may influence the future. It's how I establish credibility with my clients and myself. Because this has been an important aspect of all my readings, it disturbed me that I sometimes couldn't tell if the information was just coming from a particularly clear reading or really from the *other side.*

The truth was that I didn't know, and the whole thing fascinated me. Connecting to information about the deceased was an experience that just arrived unbidden and usually startled both my client and me. It wasn't something I could ask or look for. I always say that those who reside in the spirit world come of their own accord, in their own time, and I'm somehow given the task of translating what I receive from the impressions I get. It's up to my client to let me know if it makes sense since it has no relationship to me at all.

This also happened when I worked as an aromatherapist 19 years ago, during my transition to doing readings full-time. Aromatherapy massage was a new form of massage therapy that was just being introduced into Canada from Britain. It was based on a lymphatic-drainage technique and the use of essential oils with healing properties. I really enjoyed doing bodywork and seeing how many positive effects the treatments provided, and I had some very interesting experiences.

I once placed my hands on someone's shoulders and heard the name Joseph in my head. After the massage was over, the client looked up and said that she'd had a vision about someone named Joseph. I had five more clients in a row, and everyone said something similar:

"I think I saw a spirit guide named Joseph or Josephine."

"I kept hearing the name Joseph, and I saw a person in robes made of really bright light."

"Who is Josephine?"

"Wow, this Joseph came to me all surrounded in bright light, but I couldn't tell if the person was female or male."

At the end of the day, I spoke to the owner, who'd heard from all the clients about the strange experiences they'd had that day. He was moved to tears and awestruck. It turns out that the health center where I was working was owned by a young Italian Catholic man whose mother had passed away that day two years before. Her name was Josephina.

Another time, I was doing a treatment on a woman who told me that she'd been suffering for years from chronic lower-back pain, as well as reproductive difficulties. As soon as I put my hands on her lower body, I felt a rush of sorrow and remorse; and I heard a man's voice in my mind, telling me his name. I knew that he had molested this woman when she was a child, and he wanted to make amends. I told her what I was receiving (I was horrified!), and she jumped up. We ended up having a conversation that went past the hour allotted for her appointment.

Slightly in shock, she left healed—or so she said—but without the treatment she'd come in for. She was one of the reasons I stopped doing bodywork. It was partly because I wasn't sure how to handle the information I was getting, but mostly because people wanted to talk to me instead of getting a massage. Back in the day, that woman referred a lot of clients to me.

Still, the experience of connecting to the deceased was different from the focus of my "normal" readings. As an intuitive, my job was to impart pertinent, intimate information I received about the content and potential direction of a person's life, discussing the patterns, lessons, and trends within his or her life experience. No one came to me expecting me to be a medium; that seemed to be accidental.

Regarding communicating messages from the deceased, I always felt a little conflicted after the clients left. They seemed absolutely sure they'd received messages directly from their loved ones, leaving me just as unsure—although I nodded my head and smiled happily to have served them so well. It was obvious that the impact of the information itself was transformative, even though I felt that I couldn't legitimately claim to be sure of the source. Yet how did I know so much about the deceased unless I was able to intuit the past?

The experiences added up over the years. I described in detail how a man died of a heart attack at a client's home; and I named his widow, Charlotte, who was my client's friend. When Charlotte came to see me, I received no such message and the connection wasn't as clear. It disappointed us both, but I couldn't make it happen. I was very disconcerted, as there was an expectation on both our parts that we had a special connection, and it became obvious that we didn't. Why did her husband find it so easy to communicate to her friend but not her? I had no answer.

Today, I realize that the connection was easier because it had been made through a neutral source—a friend, not a spouse—without an emotional charge or any expectation. Sometimes wanting to connect too strongly can actually prevent it from happening. Charlotte, who had so much emotional attachment to the potential of making a connection to her husband, couldn't make the link, but her friend could. The woman who'd received the message was present when the man passed away suddenly in her home, but she wasn't looking for that experience to be discussed in her reading. It all came as a surprise.

My first editor, Janice, met me at a reading as my client, and I told her all kinds of obscure details about her deceased grandmother. She didn't know any of these facts, but they were confirmed later by her mother. Janice didn't have a clue what I was talking about, yet it was all playfully invading my mind at warp speed, and I insisted that she check to make sure I was right. Her mother said it was real, that the family was receiving information from their loved one—but again, as I had so many of these experiences for a while and then none at all, I continued to be unsure.

"I don't talk to dead people."

This was my way of protecting myself in case all of this was just my capacity to know the past, even if it wasn't in my clients' personal memory banks. Still, I was beginning to believe . . . if only a little. Many days I thought that perhaps I should look into it with a spiritualist or medium properly trained in communicating with the other side. I never found the time, but I did read a lot of books that seemed to confirm that I was indeed dialoguing with the dead. Yet since I believed it wasn't my specialty, I chose to announce to Hay House that there would be no dead people in my readings, thank you very much.

Man plans, God laughs . . . and so does everybody *over there.*

The Voyage of Voices

The first event I did with Hay House was a cruise with psychic Sylvia Browne and medium John Holland. I was terrified. Although I'd sold out full-day seminars and workshops as a teacher of metaphysics and intuition, I'd never done readings for strangers on a stage. Thank God I met John before I got started. He was (and is) a very handsome, laid-back, funny, normal guy in a baseball cap, who immediately made me feel at ease. He was so generous and kind that I was greatly relieved. I'm still thankful for him today because he made my first experience in such an environment so wonderful. I don't like being the new kid on the block, but he made it easy.

Anyhow, I was supposed to go onstage after John. I watched him at the beginning of his event and was astounded and very impressed by his accuracy and some of the similar things we taught, but I soon left because I didn't want to hear the content of his messages. I don't like to know anything about the people I'm reading, and I was concerned that I'd be influenced by what I was hearing him impart to the audience.

When my turn came, I was nervous. There were 500 interested faces, all there to absorb wisdom and receive messages—and there I was having an anxiety attack. *What if I get it wrong? In public?* So I prayed, which is my answer to everything. I became calm, although I did talk a mile a minute, trying to cram my whole life story into a short period of time.

Then it came time for the readings. These I know how to do, and it became apparent that I was on a roll. I was able to make some very accurate assessments about people in the audience, and I was enjoying myself immensely. I even set off the alarms as the audiovisual system blew out when my intuitive experience intensified energetically, which happens frequently with me. (That's a whole other story!)

Then it started happening—I began to hear voices around me and inside my mind that were saying names. I also began to sense a cool breeze around my right side, which was physically very noticeable. On my left I sensed warmth and an amazing feeling of love and compassion for me and everyone in the room. It wasn't coming *from* me; no, it was directed *to* me. Then I started feeling a sensation moving up my left side, much like the way a cat does a little push dance with its feet when it purrs. *Pad, pad, pad. Pad, pad, pad.* It was coming from the outer edges of my energy and didn't quite touch my body.

I heard and felt the words *love, love, love.*

We love you.

Thank you, we love you.

And then it started with an old lady named Ina, who chewed violet candies and spoke through me to greet her 80-year-old granddaughter, who was sitting in the back row. Someone's father showed me his clothes and a photo of himself and his favorite tractor. A husband placed a shawl around the shoulders of his young, grieving widow, who had small children; and he named a man who had taken a computer out of their house. Small, seemingly insignificant details were given to me—things that were only pertinent to those who knew the people who were coming through—and the tears kept coming. I cried with all these listeners. I felt their deep pain and knew their loneliness and grief . . . and then experienced their relief as I relayed personal and detailed information that only they could know or understand. It was just as profound for me to be a part of this as it was for them.

I delivered so many oracle messages from the other side on that cruise that I could no longer question their validity. I couldn't degrade or deny the experience, nor could I disrespect what so many were gaining from it. I was home. After many years of skepticism and inner arguing—fretting over whether the information about the deceased just existed for me to receive intuitively, or whether the immortal Spirit really was active—I'd come to an important understanding. I knew that I could indeed receive messages from those who had passed over. I came to consider myself a natural medium, as I haven't trained in the spiritualist churches like Gordon Smith (a well-known UK psychic) or John Holland. It's been my experience that a message will come through as it wants to, not because it's asked for.

Needless to say, I fired off an e-mail right quick to Reid Tracy:

> *Um, hi. I'm writing to retract my statement about what I do. It seems I do talk to dead people.*
> *I really, really get it now. Whoa.*
> *And I am humble and grateful and so very, very, sure now.*
> *Hope that's okay.*
> *I don't think I can turn it off.*
> *Okay. Gotta go, I'm needed by the other side.*
> *They sure are one talkative bunch!*

A Message from Michael

Since that time, every once in a while a reading has really affected me in a way that reminds me how powerful and transformative a message from the other side can be. I'll always remember one case because of the powerful impact it had on me in the role of *oracle messenger*.

It takes a long time to get a session with me, so most people who call get put on a waiting list for up to a year. I do get cancellations, but not very often, and when that happens, it's my assistant Michelle's job to choose someone to fill the spot. I tell her to always look at the list with intuition and her heart rather than her head, and to allow her inner voice to show her the name to call. By doing so, we always have a sense that the person is receiving a reading with perfect timing—and that's always what we end up hearing from the clients.

Michelle sent me an e-mail telling me that a woman named Deb would be replacing someone who had to change his appointment. When I was preparing for her reading, I had a sense of a young man beside me in Spirit, but I didn't pay it any mind because I'm never sure whether it's my imagination or whether it's real until I speak to my client. I only made a small mental note to review the image I was shown once I began the reading.

Once Deb and I were on the phone together, I proceeded more or less the same as always, allowing my inner vision and intuition to begin showing me a story. It took a few minutes as I adjusted my focus to the energy that was gently pushing me to see and hear the message I was to give. Deb told me at this point that she was hoping I'd be able to connect to her son, who was deceased.

I knew it was important that I do this service for Deb. I prayed to God to move my sense of limitation out of the way and asked that I receive a blessing to make the connection. Then I very clearly heard a name, repeated over and over, and I said it out loud: "Michael, Michael, Michael." Deb gasped and told me that this was, in fact, her son's name.

So many images flashed by me, and I found myself having an inner dialogue with a young man with a witty personality who found his predicament in Spirit to be almost humorous. His only concern was that his mother not worry about how he died. I got a really strong sense that he wanted his family to know that he hadn't suffered. He told me that he'd fallen off a cliff because he was startled by a rattlesnake, and he died instantly when his neck broke during the fall. Then he proceeded to show me how he was positioned when he was found. I described this to Deb, and she confirmed it.

When I'm relaying a message like this, I'm always strangely removed and without feeling, but afterward I can get very emotional. It's important for me to remain neutral, though, so I don't influence the reading with my own response. That said, I've spent many moments in tears after a reading, once I realize the magnitude of what has transpired through me to the people who come to be witnessed by my gift.

I was surprised by how clear these details were. It was as if Michael was also on the phone telling me what to share with his mom. I was so moved by the absolute certainty that the information was not only correct but also relayed through Michael's immortal consciousness. It was as if the reading—and connecting to this wonderful young man—was just as important and significant for me as it was for the immortal spirit of Michael, as well as for Deb. I'd been praying for a sign to show me that I was on the right track in becoming so public about all of this. I was truly shown the truth of Spirit and all that remains in Mystery, knowable yet unknowable in the traditional intellectual sense. These two people gave me an unforgettable gift.

This isn't about faith because of belief. It's all about faith because we *know,* and as a result of that knowing, we're able to transcend the mundane and experience the miraculous.

I invited Deb to share her story for this book in the hope that it will help others.

Deb's Story

"Michael, Michael, Michael . . ." I used to say that to my son all the time while he was growing up.

I was blessed with two wonderful children, Kristin and Michael, who grew up loving each other. While it was always important to me to love them equally, Michael was my baby. He grew up into a wonderful young man who made his mother proud; he was caring and very compassionate and had a smile that could light up a room. He was a gentle soul.

Michael would have received his degree in psychology that summer. He'd also moved back home to save money, and it was nice to have him around again. Sometimes when you think that things are going well and you have everything you need to be happy, something happens that changes your life forever. That happened to me on April 19, 2005.

I vividly remember the moment at work when I received the phone call from the Apache County Police. I couldn't figure out what the caller was trying to tell me until I realized that he was saying he was speaking to me on my son's cell phone. Then it became all too clear that something was terribly wrong. I was told that they'd found my son's car and that they believed he might have fallen. What I didn't know until later was the severity of his fall. My son, Michael Morgan, had died in an accident at the Canyon de Chelly National Monument.

Michael was on a trip to the Southwest, an area he loved. It was normal for him to call me every couple of days, and he'd done so that week to tell me what a great time he was having. If I'd only known that would be the last time I would speak to him, there are so many things I would have told him. Spirit may have known it would be our last conversation, however, because Michael ended up calling me back three times, as his cell phone kept losing the connection. He said that he kept redialing because he wanted to make sure he told me that he loved me. And in fact, the last four words he ever said to me were "I love you, Mom."

Because of the sudden, unexpected nature of Michael's accident, we were left with many unanswered questions and much remorse. What was he doing there that morning? What happened that day? How had the accident occurred? We were sad that we weren't there for him, to protect him. There were so many things we wanted to say.

I found Colette while searching the Internet. I was fixated on her picture on the front cover of <u>Remembering the Future.</u> Something made me want to find out more about this person, order her book, and make an appointment for a reading.

I was excited and happy when my one-year wait ended up being only two days. I just knew that I'd be connected to my son. I believed that he would come through in my reading with Colette, and we'd talk about him and I might feel close to him.

When the reading began, I felt as if I'd spoken to Colette many times before. We talked like best girlfriends do when catching up on old times, and she expressed the compassion of a good friend when hearing bad news.

I mentioned to her that I wanted to reach my son, at which point the reading took on a life of its own. She described his appearance and age and gave me his name. The circumstances surrounding the accident and his passing were coming in clearer and clearer. Only a person very close to me could have known these details and answers. I remember Colette telling me afterward how surprised she was and how clearly the message kept coming through for me that day.

As she began, she also said over and over, "Michael, Michael, Michael . . ."

My reading with Colette left me with a tremendous feeling of weight lifted from my shoulders, a sense of relief that my loved one is happy, safe, and still with me—but living on differently. The next day I received a "thank-you" e-mail from Colette's assistant. I froze when I noticed her name: Michelle Morgan. She shares Michael's last name and her first name is the same as one of his favorite aunts. I received what I believe to be another sign of Divine synchronicity, another connection and validation for me.

My hope in writing this message is to help one person with the grief process and provide hope that it's possible to learn to live again after a devastating loss, to honor and celebrate life. The loss of a child or sibling is something that no one should ever have to experience, nor is anyone ever prepared for it. I was lucky to have no unfinished business or unspoken feelings for my son. We had a special bond and were able to express how we felt to each other.

I love you, Michael.

CHAPTER 3

AN ORACLE
MESSAGE FOR ME

For years I never received a message from the other side; I only gave them to others. That changed when I met psychic medium and fellow Hay House author John Holland while working on that Hay House cruise in 2006 (called "A Psychic Experience at Sea"). We struck up a friendship when we found out that we shared a similar sense of humor and had a lot in common. My husband, Marc, also enjoyed John's company; and we enthusiastically committed to meeting outside of work.

When we decided to get together in Toronto in early 2007, John couldn't find a flight that worked with all our schedules, except for the weekend of February 17—the anniversary of my mother's death. When he called to tell me the date, my emotions were deeply stirred, and I took it as a sign of something important. I purposely didn't tell John the significance of that weekend because we'd casually decided that he'd give me a "sitting" (what he calls an oracle reading where he imparts messages from the living consciousness of the deceased), and I didn't want to influence him.

I was looking forward to this session with mixed emotions. I still hadn't released the nagging sense that I'd been an unworthy daughter and that I'd never be able to make up for the lost years and broken moments between my mother and me. As much as I spoke to everyone about my immense healing, this was one piece of the puzzle that I hadn't fully reconciled. What message would I receive?

Sometimes oracles come to us in profound and unexpected ways. Even when we anticipate an answer to our questions or some kind of contact, we can't possibly know how deeply we'll be affected.

Even with all my success, I'd quietly accepted that the pain regarding my mother would always just be there. I reminded myself, *Progress, not perfection.* When it came to her, I "walked my talk" with a limp and an invisible cane. I'd come to believe that something had been broken between us that could never be fully repaired. Still, I longed for peace, which was as elusive after her death as it had been while she was alive.

An Oracle Message Heals the Past

It's impossible to honor the complexities of my relationship with my parents in a few short paragraphs, but in order to share how the reading with John impacted me, I think it's important to present some background information. (I revealed some of this in my first book, *Remembering the Future,* but of course, there's so much more.) This story shows how powerful an oracle message can be if we're receptive to allowing the message to initiate healing at the heart level.

My mom and I had a tough time navigating the rough seas of our life together. I know that I scared her when I was growing up because I was so uncontrollable. In fairness to her, she came to North America to escape her past and get a fresh start in a land that promised safety, security, and opportunity. After World War II, Canada and the United States were havens for Europeans desiring new lives. She had every reason to be hopeful that turning her back on Germany and the horrible legacy that tore her family apart would let her begin anew.

Before emigrating to Canada, she was engaged to a wealthy young man who was a former SS officer. Prior to her death, she told us how she'd woken up one morning and decided that she couldn't go through with the wedding because her fiancé didn't know the truth about her. I can imagine the conflict she must have felt. She'd searched for her father in the concentration camps and finally learned that he'd been killed in Dachau. Marry an SS officer who believed she was a good Christian girl? Not a chance.

She broke off the engagement that morning, and that very afternoon got on a boat heading for Canada. She was 25 years old and knew no one there.

My mother was born a Jew, although she was hidden from the Nazis by a Christian family who later adopted her. Her father was from Paris, and he returned to France when my mom was still young, after his rocky relationship with my grandmother ended. He only came back to Berlin to find my mother and take her to safety in France; Germany was too dangerous for a young Jewish child. He was arrested by the Nazis at my mother's doorstep on her birthday. Her adoptive Christian parents told my grandfather that she was dead and were shooing him away at the time.

My mom had a lot of conflict about loyalty. Two families raised her—the modest Christians who lived just outside the city, and her wealthy Jewish grandparents who lived in town. The two sets of relatives shared the responsibilities of her upbringing, education, and safekeeping. They were equally important to her but couldn't have been more different.

Her Jewish grandparents escaped the horrors of the camps because her grandfather was a partner in the architectural firm run by Albert Speer, who was later known in the Nuremberg trials as the "Good Nazi" (not that any Nazi did anything good). He did, however, allow my great-grandparents to survive without penalty while their neighbors were taken away. My mother told us that she stood at the window on *Kristallnacht,* knowing that her family wouldn't be subjected to the horrors and feeling a deep sense of shame that such a terrible thing had happened.

My mom came to Canada to forget all of this and wipe the slate clean—to make a brand-new life with a new identity, new hopes, and new dreams. So when I was born and began to show signs of strangeness—the things that would make me different—I can see how that frightened her. It wasn't safe to stick out.

Perhaps our difficulties began when my nightmares included stories that only she could understand. I can only imagine her terror in knowing that her three-year-old daughter regularly dreamed about the worst moments of her former life—all the events she wanted to forget, the secrets she vowed no one would ever know. She must have felt anguish when she heard these very things spilling out of the mouth of her innocent child.

I can imagine the sense of intrusion and the fear she must have experienced. I can also understand her need to protect us both—herself from me and me from myself. And so the foundation of our relationship was formed on these unstable and rocky shores of emotion. I know that we shared a fierce bond of love, yet it was always threatening to break.

All through my early life, I struggled with my intuition and unusual abilities while succumbing to an eating disorder, depression, drug addiction, and alcoholism. Of course my relationship with my parents was strained. How could I have expected anything different? I know that they did the very best they could, given their own ancestral wounds, and I can only imagine the deep suffering I caused them. My mother and I were the closest, so the pain was deep for us both.

So many things happened that exacerbated our conflict. I was raped by a group of men at the same age (19) that my mother had been raped by Russian soldiers 30 years earlier, at the end of the war. And no matter how hard we tried to establish a healthy boundary, I continued to bring up the unresolved suffering of the past by repeating it in living color.

Although my experience of rape turned out to be an extraordinary gift in the end—because it allowed me to claim my intuitive abilities—it also initiated a horrendous downward spiral of self-destruction. I finally got clean and sober at age 27, but by then most of the damage had been done between my mother and me. Looking back, I guess we both got stuck there.

Even well into my sobriety and after my spiritual awakening, we were still at odds. Right until the last day she was lucid in her hospital bed, we had only one precious moment—as mother and daughter—where we just sat still, acknowledging our mutual love and our exhaustion. Still, no matter how difficult she was, I believed that our dynamic was my fault, and there was no time to make amends. Her brain cancer was swift and merciless.

I was angered by her death and by our relationship. I was mad at my father, too—he also suffered a horrible, sad, and lonely death. I was filled with rage because God let that happen and because everything was so unfair. I stayed angry because grief was too scary. I never expressed my true emotions for very long, and I managed to "numb out." I gained 60 pounds the first three months after my mother's death. *I'll show you how angry I am—I'll hurt myself.* Even though I wasn't drinking and had improved my situation immensely, I was in pain and hurting myself by eating compulsively to stuff down my feelings.

There was no more anger or sadness then, just a surrender to the distracting numbness I called healing. I used to pass out mid-sentence at my therapist's office when we spoke about my parents. I'd wake up when she said, "The session's over." She was kind and compassionate, and I needed to be there. Then over time, I stopped hurting myself and allowed what I could to be released.

And over the years, much healing did take place. I know that I worked hard and changed a lot. I wasn't ashamed any more about the rape, the psychological fallout, and my subsequent acting out. I believed that I'd forgiven everyone, made my amends, and found a life of miracles. I'd forgiven myself, too. I believed that I was completely healed from the victim consciousness of my past. That was true, but there was still something left—a nameless shame regarding my mother and father that I was always quietly aware of but rarely spoke about.

Remembering My Father

I should mention some important things about my dad, too. He was well known and respected all of his life. A successful engineer and land developer, he was also an intellectual, philosopher, inventor, and environmentalist who was active in politics. He was open to new ideas and encouraged us to educate ourselves. Most of all, my father was a proud Leo man devoted to being a provider.

One of our family's best memories was when he was invited to present a paper at a world conference in Stockholm, Sweden, on environmental issues. He was talking about windmill power, electric cars, and solar energy in 1966. He believed that global warming could potentially be disastrous, and he wanted to see environmental change—and this was 40 years ago. He was definitely a man ahead of his time.

The first part of my life was privileged because of my father. He made it possible for my sister and me to attend elite private schools and to enjoy fancy cars, fur coats (I'd never wear one now!), and yearly trips to Europe. His name opened doors that were closed to others.

But that wasn't how I came to remember him. Somehow, tragedy managed to erase the good and replace those memories with what came later. I've seen this in my clients, too. Loss can be a strong force that blindfolds us and holds the good things in life hostage.

When my dad died on February 2, 1991, he was penniless and broken. He lost everything in an unfair business deal when he was 75 years old—even our house was taken away. My family lived on the sale of the leftover antiques, paintings, and collectibles that were sold at ridiculous prices . . . and my mother's $8-an-hour job at a secondhand-clothing store.

My father never recovered. We watched him slowly die for eight years as he lost his will to live. Alzheimer's disease and his own sense of failure brought him down. My mother followed right after him, felled by a malignant brain tumor.

A Personal Reading

It's clear why I was nervous about John Holland reading for me, yet I was hoping for confirmation that all was well on the other side and that my parents were able to hear me. My questions were the same ones I've whispered to them daily, alone in my prayers: "Are you okay? Are you happy? Do you know my heart aches and how sorry I am, even after all these years? Do you forgive me? Are you proud of what I've become?"

Did you think my concerns would be more profound than those of any other person looking for answers through a psychic or medium just because I am one myself? No lofty existential inquiries from me. I didn't care what heaven looked like or whether the Divine matrix or a "multi-verse" were real. I just wanted to know the answers to those questions. The oracle message I sought was deeply personal.

The day before John was supposed to arrive, Oprah Winfrey had psychic mediums John Edward and Allison DuBois on her show. Allison, whose life inspired the hit television series *Medium,* presented herself in such a highly credible way that I was very impressed. Scientist Dean Radin made his case, however briefly, about how science is proving that all human beings have a higher sensory perception and that our consciousness may, in fact, be eternal. Beyond my excitement that Oprah's show lent more credibility to my profession (due to her influence in the world), I saw it as a personal sign that I was ready to connect to my parents.

When John arrived, he was clearly exhausted, so we moved at a relaxing pace. I realized that I had to let go of my desire for a reading. The last thing I wanted was to put pressure on him when he so obviously wasn't into doing anything more than chilling at home with Marc and me. I was curiously relieved. I had the unsettling thought that maybe my parents wouldn't come through anyway—and what then? So much for the "Oprah sign."

That weekend was a lot of fun, and included taking John to visit our friends who claimed to have a haunted house. Although no ghosts that we could actually "see" attended the party, everyone definitely felt a strange presence and went home worn-out. I couldn't sleep at all that night, so I lay there wondering about my parents, especially my mom.

No one could have planned what happened next. The evening of the 17th, the anniversary of my mother's passing, John and I went into my cozy office where we just naturally began doing what we do. I decided to read for him, and he started scribbling. I thought he was listening to my wisdom (it was a good reading) and was fervently writing down every word I said. It seemed a little strange that he was writing so quickly and using both sides of the piece of paper—but then again, what made me think either one of us was so normal? Hello?

Never mind what I saw for him, because it turned out that he was getting impressions about my parents. They were there.

Then something powerful began to happen. All of a sudden I saw a faint, fuzzy light behind John; and my normally quiet little dog, Beanie, started going nuts and barking at the air between us.

"John, can you see it? Can you see it?" I asked.

Beanie was barking with so much anxiety, following the fuzzy light that moved slowly around us before disappearing. But the dog was still seeing something! I had to calm her down as John began to relay what he was receiving.

My dad came through first, and he wanted me to see him in a tuxedo. His appearance was important to him. He talked (through John) about only having wanted to be a provider for his family.

My heart ached, even though I was excited, because he'd often said those specific words. Oh, and in my favorite picture of him . . . he's wearing a tux. I understand why he wanted to be wearing such nice clothes when he communicated with me. He was in heaven, on top of his game again.

John went on to relay things about my father that he couldn't possibly know. I wrote at length about my family in *Remembering the Future,* but none of this information was in it. John talked about my father's political history during World War II, when he worked as a spy for the British. Dad was an engineer and told us that he'd built bridges for the Germans, then blown them up for the British.

John saw that my dad was in a jail-like place twice. Once, he was imprisoned for an attempt on Mussolini's life. The second time was when the Russians, who thought he was working for the Germans, had captured him. He was tortured for days and was almost killed before the Brits saved him. John was also given impressions of my father's involvement in Canadian politics later in life.

That was definitely my dad. No sappy "I love you" from him—instead, he wanted me to remember all the things he was proud of. I'd been stuck for so long in recalling those difficult later years. I just remembered his powerlessness, and he was reminding me that it wasn't always that way.

For the first time, my heart heard a message that broke the spell of my sordid memories. I'd forgotten all the good. I was shocked and deeply moved.

Then my mom came through, and John wrote down her essence in a few sentences. He saw her as she was: physically beautiful, complex, vivacious, in control at all times, and a lover of animals. She was a survivor. The Holocaust may have destroyed her family, but it didn't break her spirit. She'd never been that vulnerable again. Just as she'd changed countries, she also switched religions. Like her, Jesus started out as a Jew, and I guess she figured that what was good enough for Jesus was good enough for us. So I grew up as Christian, loving Christ—or at least what he represented.

I saw John write: "My darling Colette" in handwriting like my mom's. Then he looked at me and calmly said, "Your mother is telling me that when you found the letter, she was behind you and with you."

My mom had written me a letter that she'd put with some photos she'd preserved before her death. I'd found it in a box just a few months earlier, and I'd spent some time that day on my knees and in tears. *Why can't I move past this? What am I missing?* I'd wondered. John couldn't possibly have known that I'd found a letter from my mom—one that began: "My darling Colette."

"She loves you very much," John went on. "She's so glad you think of her, and she wants your forgiveness."

She wants your forgiveness.

I was dumbstruck. Although there were lots of details proving that John was really making contact with my parents, this one was the most meaningful to me. This was the key to the door I'd never been able to open.

And so the transformative power of the oracle began to take shape around me. Time slowed down and my senses became acute as I was poised to listen more deeply than I ever had before. When an oracle is true, the entire body vibrates like a string on a harp. All the chaos begins to have a pattern that makes sense—as if all questions have been answered for the very first time, even the ones that haven't been asked yet.

With his last statement, John imparted an oracle so rich with healing that I couldn't speak about it for a couple of days. Marc asked me if I wanted to talk about it, but I couldn't.

I'd spent so many years pleading for forgiveness, but I'd never thought to forgive my mother. It never occurred to me that I hadn't. (The truth was that I hadn't really forgiven myself either.) I now understood that I was the one keeping us both stuck, when we should have moved on ages ago.

Yet I was a walking miracle. I'd healed from the trauma of rape. I'd embarked on a spiritual path and had been clean and sober for almost 22 years, taking it one day at a time. I had a happy marriage and my life was a success. I'd changed so much that no one from my early years could recognize me. Still, this crucial piece of my life had been left behind. This was the fundamental key to what was missing within me.

The reading with John was so profound that any description pales in comparison to its true impact on me. In receiving his oracle message, I felt that I was finally given permission to heal.

In *Remembering the Future,* one of my seven keys to recovering intuition is Forgiveness. I believe that this is one of the most important aspects of spiritual growth and healing. I guess we teach what we need to learn—and I had no idea how much more I needed to do.

Until John sat with me and became the conduit for the souls of my parents, I'd only been able to go so deep and so far. Now I could fly.

Confirmation

John told me that I might begin to doubt the experience so that my parents might come through again in another form. Synchronicities are another way in which Spirit brings us awareness.

When I read for someone onstage, sometimes a message also has meaning for another person in the audience. Countless times, people have approached me when I'm signing books after an event to tell me excitedly that what I said to someone else applied to them and they're so thankful. When Spirit uses an innocent speaker to impart a message such as this to someone, unbeknownst to them, it's called a *Cledon*. This oracle tradition dates back to ancient Rome (which I'll discuss more later in this book).

It was my turn to experience that synchronicity. During a reading I did on the Tuesday after John left, another oracle was given to me. This client, a successful entrepreneur, had been coming to me every year since 1995. We normally spoke about his business, but that day was different. We talked about his new love, for he felt that he'd found his match. In the course of the conversation, he mentioned that his sweetheart shared his birthday, and he'd never met anyone else with that date—January 31.

This was a Cledon! My mother's birthday was the 31st, too. I told him about my mom and my own reading, and we sensed that something profound was going on for both of us. I carried on with his session, excited about the synchronicity. Then I casually asked what his girlfriend's name was. He said, "Her name is Eva."

My mom's name was Eva.

It took about a week for me to process the depth of the oracle message. The information wouldn't have had the same impact coming from any other source. If a therapist told me that my mom would have wanted my forgiveness and that I needed to release the self-sabotaging identity of a flawed, undeserving daughter, it wouldn't have had the same effect.

The ways in which I received the message—through the extraordinarily accurate and compassionate mediumship of John Holland, the fuzzy light, my dog barking at nothing, and the synchronicity of the reading a few days later—all served a higher purpose. I couldn't deny this, and I had to address all of it. It was time. I was free at last to really grieve, and I understood the potential of transformation that oracles bring. I received what I've been so blessed to give others.

Spirit, Broccoli, and a Little Yellow Trike

Here's another story concerning the connection between parents and children. When I was on the road for the *Spiritual Connections* tour, one day I kept having a craving for Chinese broccoli. I'd been told that the Chinese name for the vegetable was *kai-lan,* so I heard that word in my mind when I thought of the broccoli steaming on my plate. The unusual name would prove to be a key to a transformative Spirit message I received for a woman named Madge.

Marc had asked me to do a favor for Madge. She was one of the certified LifeLine practitioners, working with Hay House author Dr. Darren Weissman, and she'd recently lost her son. Marc had spent time with her at a couple of conferences and was deeply impressed by her.

He asked if I could possibly pick up something about her son when she attended the *Spiritual Connections* tour in Nashville. Marc didn't tell me the boy's name, but did say that he'd been killed by a drunk driver.

I didn't think I'd be able to read for Madge because I was under the impression that there's an adjustment period after someone passes away—in other words, it takes a few months before a person's consciousness is active again on the other side. My mediumship skills were raw and untrained, and I was pretty sure I wouldn't be able to make contact. I was sorry that I would disappoint her, but I accepted it. And I still invited her to meet me backstage before the event began.

Before I go onstage, I always pray for Spirit to use me to help whoever needs assistance. As soon as I began my prayer that night, my mind was flooded with memories that weren't mine. First, I saw an SUV and images of wheels of all shapes and sizes. I saw someone with a sudden and painful head injury that seemed as if the skull was bruised and cracked. I felt something like a clap of thunder inside of me, then a floating peaceful feeling. Next, I saw myself under a truck or car, looking up at a dirty engine.

The two images that followed were strange and insistent. I saw a big yellow-plastic tricycle with a bright yellow seat. And I saw Chinese broccoli—huh?

Oh well, I thought. *Maybe I'll get Chinese takeout after the event.*

None of the images meant anything to me at that point, and they could have belonged to any of the ten people who might be called to the stage for a reading.

Then Madge was brought backstage to meet me. I walked over to her, and all the scenes from my prayer came flooding back. I told her what I'd seen, and she confirmed that it all applied to her son. I saw that he'd had a love of trucks that began when he got his yellow trike. I knew that he'd died instantly and hadn't suffered.

While she was standing there, I also picked up the consciousness of an alcoholic man, who I immediately knew to be Madge's deceased father. I got an impression of words and feelings (rather than hearing an actual voice) filled with sincerity and a desire to make amends and to nurture his family—although that hadn't been possible in the past. Her dad seemed to be saying: "I'm so sorry I wasn't there for you, but now I can look after your son."

Madge seemed slightly stunned and said that her father had died some 30 years previously. And then she told me that her son's name was Kylen.

We hugged, and both of us were moved by the exchange. Then I pulled away. I needed to disconnect so that I could be as detached as possible when I went onstage.

Before she left, however, Madge handed me a card with a metal bookmark in it, which I decided I would look at more closely when I got back to the hotel. The card read:

> *Faith sees the invisible,*
> *Believes the incredible,*
> *And receives the impossible.*

When I sat down to write about this, the significance of the Chinese broccoli suddenly occurred to me: *kai-lan . . .* Kylen. Here's what Madge had to say about it:

> *After the weekend when I met Colette, friends began calling me with stories of having heard from Kylen in some way. I even received word from someone in Oregon, whom I hadn't talked to in 15 years—this professional intuitive heard my son during a meditation. Also, while my friend Deborah was cooking dinner after I'd been at her house, she heard him say, "My mom used to make that." One night my next-door neighbor asked if I wanted to walk our dogs together. After we'd been walking for a few minutes she said, "I don't know if I should tell you this or not, but Kylen's been talking to me."*
>
> *But the experience with Colette was simply incredible—a story that we can all believe in. I rushed home after seeing her and dug out the photos of Kylen on his third birthday, when he was helping his dad build that yellow trike. I looked at his little face as he was squatting down and watching how the first big wheel went into place, and I saw his concentration while twisting a screwdriver in another shot. What a treasure! Can you believe I actually have pictures? In showing Colette the trike, Kylen must have known that I needed something tangible to have as proof so my heart could be happy about his adventures beyond the veil, in the "real world."*

I'm also incredibly grateful to know that my father had been trying to get in contact with me for years and that he's seeking to make amends for the issues we experienced. And I'm especially glad that he'll keep an eye out for his marvelous grandson.

CHAPTER 4

ANIMALS AS ORACLE MESSENGERS

Our companion animals aren't just important to us as pets to love and cuddle; they also serve an oracular purpose, although we often don't know how to see it. In fact, they're the most accurate mirrors of our starting point for a conscious dialogue with Spirit. This is their main purpose in choosing to spend time with us. They come to facilitate our spiritual growth in a mutual, evolving, dynamic relationship. They act as our constant sacred sign-bearers connecting us daily to the language of oracles, omens, and signs.

Wild animals, even those we encounter in urban settings, are also powerful oracles and sacred sign-bearers. In many respects, they're the first living oracle messengers in human history. For this reason I've devoted an entire chapter to the furry, feathered, and scaly creatures that Spirit sends us as Divine messengers.

I was born to love and protect animals. I was surrounded by them growing up—the rodents my mom carried in her apron pockets, the birds flying around the house, and all the beloved dogs that barked and slobbered. We always had a wild animal that my mom was bringing back to health so that we could place it gently back into the wild. My mother nursed a baby raccoon with an eyedropper until her eyes opened. I fell in love with her on the spot when we found her in the chimney, and we named her Petunia.

I just always believed that animals, birds, and other living creatures had souls and were somewhat wiser and more dignified and
authentic than humans. Most important, I saw the same glowing
lights around them that I saw around the saints in the stained-
glass windows at church. I knew that the halos meant the animals
were holy, too. In fact, all my companion dogs came to me in the
same way—through dreams and strange, obvious synchronicities
that always reminded me that their presence fulfilled a larger holy
spiritual contract with me.

G'dog, Gizmo!

The way in which these animals arrived showed me that Spirit
didn't just send me signs, but practically put up billboards to get
me to pay attention. For instance, Gizmo, my mischievous Maltese, was committed to letting me know who was okay to have
in the house and who wasn't. Once, when I was still doing aromatherapy at home, a man came to me for a massage treatment.
After taking one look at this client, Gizmo started attacking one
of his dog toys. He stared at me, then at the man, and back at me,
clearly letting me know he didn't approve of this person's energy.
Then he did the most hysterical thing.

Gizmo got a roll of toilet paper and ran full tilt around and
around the massage table, unraveling the roll. I did everything in
my power not to laugh, but I couldn't help myself. The man let me
know he hated dogs, and I asked him to leave, no need to pay. I
couldn't stop laughing. There was Gizmo with toilet paper around
his head and body. Plus, there was that big white "rope" all around
the massage table!

I wasn't laughing a couple of weeks later, however, when I
found out that my erstwhile client had been charged with assault
and battery. He'd been jailed for the forcible confinement of his
former girlfriend. Gizmo was letting me know that this man wasn't
safe. After that, I always paid attention when my little dog sent me
his thoughts about people.

My next dog was Trinket, a little Yorkshire terrier. After I got her home, I discovered that she was incontinent. What was I going to do with a dog that needed a diaper like a baby? I made one—that's what I did. She was a patient little creature and stood stoically so I could experiment like a mad diaper professor. My first attempt was made from a maxi pad sewn into a newborn's diaper that I cut to fit her. The cover was leopard-print flannel.

I took Trinket everywhere, even to Europe. Alert and very smart, she'd tilt her head and cock one of her "feathered" ears when I spoke to her. With an uncanny sense of the world, she was truly a sacred sign-bearer in my life, acting as a miniature warning system. She'd even alert me that the phone was going to ring and barked ten minutes before anyone arrived at my door.

After she'd been with me for several years, I planned a vacation without her. A few days before I was supposed to leave, I'd "thrown" the tarot cards and gotten a clear indication that there would be a death around me soon. Whenever a reading pulls the Ace of Swords with the Death card and a face card, it always portends a death. The face card I pulled was the Page of Cups, which meant a young girl. I was scared and anxious because I couldn't tell who it meant. Could I prevent this by knowing? I wrote about it in my journal and confided in a couple of my girlfriends. Nothing resonated as being the answer, however, so I decided it was a fluke and let it go.

The trip wasn't relaxing because I kept mulling over what I'd seen in the cards. I was on high alert and couldn't enjoy the beautiful Jamaican spa I was visiting. I kept having sad dreams where I was crying and running to stop something that I couldn't prevent from happening.

I got home to find that my little Trinket had been killed by another dog in a freak accident. Nothing could have prevented it. I knew it was no one's fault, as my friend who was taking care of her loved her and would never have put her in danger. From what I was told, she practically leapt into the jaws of a golden retriever who killed her instantly with one fatal bite. I was totally distraught with grief and guilt at having left her.

Then a week after she died, Trinket came to me in a dream. In pictures and feelings, she conveyed that I'd proven that I was capable of giving unselfish love and extreme care to a sentient being in need. She "told" me that she'd done her part by watching over me, but she needed to return to Spirit. By the time she died, she had cancer and was worried that I would have let her get sicker, thinking that keeping her alive meant my love for her was strong. She was ready to go. I told Trinket how much my heart broke because of her loss and how much I missed her. She flooded me with feelings of love.

Exactly three weeks to the day after Trinket's death, I woke up to a light shining in my face. It was the moon, fuller and brighter than I'd noticed in a while. I got out of bed and went into the living room, where I noticed an indentation on Trinket's pillow. That wasn't possible! I'd fluffed that pillow the day before, knowing I would have to eventually throw it out since it had a strong smell of urine. But at that moment, it smelled like it had been on the clothesline outside in a breeze. It was clean and fresh—not at all the way it had been before.

Wide awake by that point, I started thinking about getting another dog. I was drawn to Pomeranians, as I kept thinking about a friend's two dogs of that breed. So that night, I Googled "Pomeranian" and chose a kennel that made aromatherapy products for dogs. I'd been an aromatherapist, and that connection was my first nudge.

Then I read: "For sale: female, two years old, name . . . Trinket. Posted February 12, 12 P.M. mountain standard time." I gasped. My Trinket died at 2 P.M. eastern standard time on February 12.

This was no coincidence. I paced around my apartment, waiting until it was 7 A.M. in the kennel's time zone to call them. I babbled away about Trinket and all the signs and omens and Spirit's will—I must have sounded like a complete fruitcake! I even offered to drive there "right now, today, because God says that's my dog." But the trip would have taken four days—or longer—since it was the dead of winter. The kennel staff said they would ship her to me.

When she arrived, she slid out of her traveling kennel like a funny little red fox with a big bushy blonde tail. She licked me immediately, looked into my eyes, and started making the most hilarious noises. She sounded like a Tribble from the old *Star Trek* TV series. Instead of barking "ruff ruff," she emitted a high-pitched "rrrreeee rrrreeee."

Like all my other dogs, this Trinket also had a sickness that wasn't apparent when she'd been sent to me; it appeared two weeks after she arrived. She developed a collapsed trachea, which isn't uncommon for this breed. But a visit to my vet revealed something horrible: Trinket's vocal cords had been cut, which devastated me when I realized that the funny Tribble-like sounds coming from her expressive little face were the result of the operation. Regardless, she was a talkative little dog, and her condition didn't stop her from vocalizing. She merrily squeaked along, not caring that she sounded like a puppy on helium.

I called the kennel, and they told me her former trainer had had her "de-barked," a procedure for show dogs that make too much noise. So as well as the collapsed trachea, she also had scar tissue in her tiny throat from the removal of her vocal cords. I had a sinking feeling that she wouldn't be with me for long.

And I was correct. It was the nature of our contract. I was able to give Trinket the care she needed as she helped heal my heart and taught me more about life, compassion, responsibility—and most important—the continuation of love. Oh, and she made it clear that she didn't want to be called Trinket, since the name was awkward for us both. I renamed her Tinkerbelle, and she liked the nickname Tinky.

She also sent another kind of sign to me. Every time she squeaked, I felt a pang of loss for her voice. I came to realize that I, too, had lost my voice. I'd given up on my singing career and had even relinquished the desire to sing altogether. I felt as though I'd lost my capacity to truly express who I was in the world. My work as an intuitive needed something to give me balance, but I hadn't reconciled the fact that I allowed myself to accept the silence.

A few months later, I was given an opportunity to fly to Los Angeles to work with producer Eric Rosse on some music, which became the album *Magdalene's Garden,* and I relaunched my career on the EMI record label. At the ripe young age of 42, I began singing again and rediscovered my voice. Tinkerbelle taught me that I needed to find it.

She was only with me for a year and a half before she succumbed to complications from the combination of the scar tissue in her throat and the collapsed trachea. She died in my arms, unable to breathe but knowing she was loved and always heard by me.

Spirit Messengers Wear Fur

My dogs have all been constant reminders of the divinity and intelligence within all sentient beings. As beloved companions, they've performed a sacred service by showing me that Spirit is everywhere, not just inside me. They remind me that all relationships are mirrors to gaze into so we can grow and be who we're meant to be. They show me the beauty of remaining fully in the present without judgment. They show me how to be. They remind me that "the All is forever in the small."

In all of their deaths, they've given me the ultimate opportunity to feel reconciled and alive, without the numbness that isolates us in our modern world. The pain of their loss has helped me really understand gratitude and grace. They've helped break my heart wide open. I've become more compassionate and have learned the deeper connections that can so easily be forgotten when we're self-centered and not present in the moment. They've given me a taste of God in every breath they shared with me.

Marc and I now live with two other Pomeranians: Sebastian and Beanie. As you may have gathered, I'm a dog person—but don't get me wrong, it's not because I don't love cats. In fact, I would have ten cats if I could, but my asthma pushes me to honor my lifetime contract with canines. I think I exhausted my feline connection in my past lives serving as a priestess in the cat temples of Egypt. So as not to shortchange our feline companions, however, let me tell you about my friend Jill Kramer's kitten.

Little Man and the Case of Mistaken Identity

When Jill's beloved cat Sage crossed over at age 19, it was a painful and sad parting. Sage had come to Jill just as she was making a life change, and the arrival of this extraordinary (and highly evolved) creature marked the turning point in her spiritual awakening and choice of practice. Sage had been a beloved companion to Jill and her other cat, 15-year-old Dolly, and the emptiness left by her passing was excruciating. Jill decided to get another cat, mostly because we both believed it was possible that the original Sage would return in the body of a new kitten.

When a litter of kittens was ready for adoption, Jill was drawn to a male black-and-white tabby, although Sage had been a female. Many of her friends, myself included, encouraged her to choose this particular cat. Jill decided to call him Mr. Sage. I had a strong intuition that this cat belonged to Jill and, as I wanted her to be happy, I also wanted this kitten to be "Sage returned."

Well . . . maybe . . . but maybe not. As time passed, Mr. Sage began to act out like Jekyll and Hyde in a feline fur suit. One minute he was a hilarious, affectionate companion and the next he was a little Tasmanian devil. He took to attacking and mounting poor diabetic Dolly. Jill started to realize that this wasn't Sage returned at all, but she loved the little guy anyway. It was obvious that this kitten had *chosen* her, but who was he really, and how was she going to restore peace in the house?

Feeling guilty for my part in the "Sage is back" debacle, I gave Jill a present for her birthday: a reading from animal clairvoyant and natural healer extraordinaire Christine Agro. Jill was completely astounded by the accuracy of the reading. Christine mentioned that Mr. Sage "told her" that he didn't like his name and wanted to be called something else. Jill realized that he wanted to be appreciated for himself, and not expected to be a reincarnation of another cat. Meanwhile, Jill tried to think of another name. For some reason, "Little Man" came to mind, but she wasn't sure about it, and she relayed all of this to me later that day.

On a subsequent day, I read for a woman in Chicago. I really liked her and had a sense that there was something about her that could be meaningful, but I couldn't get a clear vision of why. I chalked it up to enjoying her personality. Suddenly, I began thinking of Jill's cat, who seemed to be "scratching at my mind," for me to pay attention. I frequently connect with spirits that come as symbolic oracle messengers on behalf of my clients. This time, rather than interpreting the cat to mean independence, needing to set boundaries, and so on, I felt compelled to ask this woman, "Do you have a cat?"

She replied, "Yes, Little Man." Wow!

I took this as a clear sign from Jill's cat that he wanted to be called Little Man, so I called her after the reading to tell her so. She was out to lunch, so I left a message. Later, she told me that at the exact time I'd left the message, she was driving in her car, thinking, *Yup, his name is Little Man. I know he wants to be called Little Man.*

Of course, the former Mr. Sage is now a happy Little Man!

(And maybe his big sister Dolly will reap the benefits of his newfound happiness!)

~≈⟨⟩≈~

While dogs and cats are the most popular companion animals, you're about to meet a whole bunch of others who serve as oracle messengers. Animals in the wild, our companion animals, and humans are here to fulfill a Divine sacred purpose. We're all filled with the individuated spark of Divine intelligence. We're sons and daughters of Spirit, filled with and surrounded by this Awareness, connecting and intertwining inside and outside time and space. Inherent in this dance is a power too great to measure. We may be unaware of the part we play on behalf of others, but Spirit always knows where to lead us to learn and grow.

When we remember this and open up our hearts without judgment, perhaps we'll recall the most important aspect of our existence—that we were placed here as custodians of this sacred world. Maybe we'll remember how to be good caregivers for this world instead of the destructive and intrusive force that we've become (even though we may believe that we have good and progressive intentions).

The truth is that even if we're undeserving and the planet seems to be dying, the creatures of the earth, sea, and sky wait for us to notice that Spirit is everywhere. When we do so, they can pick up the conversation we lost long ago. They want to be our sacred sign-bearers and to have relationships with us. I know the magic is waiting, and Spirit knows, too. We all need to experience the world as being more than just physical. We must begin to "behave as if the God in all life matters."

It's not difficult either. Within each of us is the ancestral memory of how our nonhuman fellows have served us—symbolically and interpersonally—since the beginning of time. We have the ability to remember that we all come from the God behind all gods.

We can each tap into the frequency that facilitates interspecies communication, which will help us grow and guide us on our journeys. Once we can tune in, we'll be amazed by how all of Nature is chattering away, just waiting to be heard and understood. Animals aren't silent now—nor have they ever been. They know what's up in our world and are invested in helping us remember who we are.

One afternoon I meditated and asked for a sign as to who would like to share an animal story to help illustrate these points, and I kept getting an image of a magpie. Then I thought about Christine Agro (**www.healingdog.com**), who helped me deal with my perceived role in my dogs' poor health.

Christine has made a big impact on me, my animals, and this book. She's a truly gifted, clairvoyant, natural healer with a unique approach to animal health, wellness, and spiritual understanding. After working with thousands of animals (including mine), she's become an advocate for the rights of these creatures, supporting their natural healing abilities; speaking on their behalf; and conveying their needs, wishes, and desires. She is—beyond a doubt—the real deal, and I can attest to her service.

Because of her deep and intimate relationships with the animal kingdom, I knew Christine had many stories to share about her experiences with animals, both in the wild and at home, acting as oracle messengers and sacred sign-bearers. I called her, and we enthusiastically spoke about animal stories and mutually found the connection to the magpie. I asked her if she would share that story for this book, and she happily agreed to do so (as well as contributing another story, too).

The Rescue

When I first moved to Denver, Colorado, in 1997, I had four dogs in my life. The youngest was a female Shar-Pei we called Pebbles. She was a funny dog. I was convinced that she saw out-of-body Spirits and would spend hours following them around our house. At least with her around I always knew where the Spirits were! I could sense them, too. One day Pebbles was lying at the closed sliding-glass door that led to the balcony. A magpie landed on the balcony and looked in the window at the dog, and she just lay there staring back. Every day the two animals took to looking at each other in this way. Never surprised by what Pebbles was doing, I just enjoyed this odd relationship. Little did I know that she was forging a most important link to the outside world.

I had a habit of hiking on my own when I lived in Colorado. I know people always say to never hike alone, but I always felt safe and protected by Nature and the Universe. One day I somehow stumbled off the trail; it was getting late, and I knew I was lost. Panic set in for a moment, and then I grounded myself and requested help, saying: "I am lost, and I need some direction to get back to the trailhead."

Moments later, a magpie arrived and landed in a tree several yards away, in the opposite direction from where I was headed. I prepared to continue walking the path I was on, when the magpie called. I turned and asked, "Are you talking to me?" It flew off by two trees, again in the opposite direction, and it waited. So I headed toward it and this continued: As I got close, it flew forward by several trees. I followed the magpie until it led me to the trailhead. As the destination came into sight, the bird gave a great call and flew off.

I don't think it was a coincidence that Pebbles's friend was a magpie, and that's who arrived to help me.

The Benediction

My life is dedicated to helping, healing, and speaking for animals. Because of this, the animal world sends me support and guidance and congratulates me when I have a breakthrough that's important for the animal kingdom.

As an iridologist (an expert in using the iris of the eye to find indications of bodily health and disease), I use my knowledge to help dogs. After amassing documentation on the effective use of iridology with canines, I finally decided to take my information to the public and arranged to speak at an animal massage and bodyworkers conference that was being held in Toledo, Ohio. When I landed at the Toledo airport, I arranged for a car to take me to the hotel. We had to use a highway that ran through a rural area; there were lots of trees and the road wasn't too busy. The next part happened in a bit of blur, but here's how I remember it:

Out of the corner of my eye, I saw a wolf exit the forest on the opposite side of the highway. He ran out across the lanes to the median and reached the side window of the car just as we drove by. I saw him look in the window at me—I saw his eyes as they met mine. As we passed, he ran behind the car, looking back over his shoulder before continuing into the woods. The driver exclaimed, "We never see wolves around here!"

There were several reasons why this experience was so meaningful for me. First, wolves are guardians. Second, I consider them to be the granddaddies of the canine, and finally, they have a strong connection to psychic energy and insight. The wolf brought me a greeting, a blessing, and a gift to acknowledge the importance of my work and the step I was taking. He reminded me that powerful energies were there to support me.

Don't Leave Out the Horse, of Course

Although horses can be considered companion animals, there's a distinct "otherness" about them because they serve us in very different ways from the dogs, cats, or other domestic animals that share our homes. All of the "horse people" I've ever spoken to agree with me. Horses stand on their own in their relationship with us. They have their own brand of loyalty, intelligence, and majesty that can never be questioned. We're changed forever once we've looked into the dark liquid pools of their eyes deep enough to see our own soul inside of theirs. When they make a connection with us, they remain within us, as this next story will show.

I met Juli at a seminar I held in San Francisco. I was struck by her transformative stories of how animals have acted as her oracle messengers, guiding her deep and personal transformation. Here's her story about her horse Bluestem.

Bluestem and the Broodmares

I've always loved horses. Even as a toddler, my favorite companion was a dappled-gray rocking horse named Apple Jay, whose rolling back carried me safely to enchanted lands beyond the reach of my family's drunken discord. It was no surprise that the first thing I did when I grew up was buy a horse— a gray horse.

His name was Bluestem, and he was pewter gray with the noblest of arching necks, warm brown eyes, and a petal-soft muzzle. We shared a unique bond. He was my steadfast and generous teacher, gently tolerating my mistakes and lack of self-confidence. He taught me to trust myself, and in his tenderness I felt the very grace of God.

Although I learned to fear my own species while growing up, I instinctively trusted animals without reservation. My constrained relationships with people made it hard to separate what was happening inside my head—my internal reality— from what was outside in the "real" world. So I often denied my feelings, exchanging them for an uneasy pantomime of what I thought I should feel and do.

Self-abnegation takes its toll. By the age of 27, I was tired and took chemical shortcuts to resolve my increasing anxiety. Bluestem knew that, too. I decided to move from my childhood home in Iowa to California, and I realized that I couldn't take Bluestem with me. I feared I wouldn't be able to support either one of us and made the heart-wrenching decision to sell him to a friend. It has taken many years for me to reconcile with that choice and its outcome.

I'd been in California for three years when I awoke one night from a sound sleep. I sat bolt upright in utter terror, convinced that Bluestem was dying. This feeling was undeniable and wretched—a sinking, cold vacuum in my chest. I didn't know what had happened, didn't have any images or events in mind, just the horrible feeling. I tried to dismiss it as a bad dream, but it wouldn't go away. Unable to sleep, I tossed and turned until first light, unusually grateful to get out of bed and go off to work.

Throughout the morning, I grew increasingly obsessed with concern for Bluestem. I told myself I was nuts, that even if something had happened to him I could do nothing about it, that he wasn't my horse anymore. Still, none of that self-talk settled my soul, and I finally tried to call Bluestem's new mom. Her number had been disconnected. Driven then, I tried to get in touch with other people. Increasingly frantic, I called everyone I knew, finally reaching a mutual friend who boarded her horse at the same stable as Bluestem. I'll never forget her first words:

"Oh my God, you must have heard. How did you hear?"

My stomach lurched. She confirmed my dream, saying they'd put Bluestem down about ten minutes before my call. She told me that he'd been shot the previous night in the pasture he shared with several other horses—shot in the back and left to die. They found him in the morning and determined he couldn't be saved, so they chose to put him down.

Bluestem was killed Labor Day weekend of 1994, after which I felt as though I lost my mind. Anguish that I'd sold him, guilt that I couldn't help when he'd clearly reached out to me, anger that he'd been mercilessly shot and had suffered— were all unbearable. I didn't want to live in a world where such things could happen. That I had felt and known what happened —despite distance, time, and our changed relationship— was undeniable evidence of a persistent connection that I couldn't explain but had failed to heed.

I went to live on a horse-breeding ranch in Wilton, California, as a working student, basically performing unpaid labor in exchange for board and training for my horses and me. The animals at Wilton were broodmares and foals, and they lived uninterrupted in their fields most of the time. Twice per year they came in: once to be impregnated and once to foal. Otherwise, they were left to their own society. Unlike with riding horses, I entered their world, not the other way around. Broodmares know exactly who you are and what you're capable of, and I didn't take care of them—they took care of me. It's an honor to be accepted by a herd, and by taking me in, they saved my life.

After I left Wilton, the mares and Bluestem remained with me in some way. Today, my spiritual connection to animals is something I nurture rather than medicate or hide. I honor my feelings, and I act on them. I've become an advocate rather than an animal "owner," and I dedicate all I can to the care, rescue, and rehabilitation of those creatures who need help.

My journey is a testament to the power of healing between human and animal spirits. That transformative connection has provided my purest joy, gravest sorrow, ultimate redemption . . . and now my life's work.

Insect Messages

While birds, wolves, and horses all have a certain majesty about them, I have a funny story of my own about our lowly insect friends, their role as sign-bearers, and how communication with them is not only possible but amazingly effective. Late one fall I moved into my best friend Ruth's apartment in a Victorian walk-up. It had old wooden floors and wainscoting on the walls. Where the two met, there were spaces from years of the wood warping. Although the unit was cleaned thoroughly before anyone moved in, it was one of those places where dust bunnies love to make their home—and those gaps between the floor and baseboards just beckoned for tenants. That said, we were pretty vigilant about keeping it clean, especially because I was squeamish about bugs.

I remember the day of reckoning well. I'd been working full-time as an intuitive for about five years, but I still wanted to be somebody else. I woke up one morning concerned that I couldn't handle the stress of doing readings. I was conflicted about my profession now that it was flourishing, and my career in music was floundering. I was also dealing with my mother's brain-cancer diagnosis and was having a terrible time emotionally. I kept dreaming that I was right in the middle of all these different scenarios: a tsunami, a hurricane, a volcanic explosion, a tidal wave, and a meteor crash. I always woke up terrified that I didn't know how to survive in my own life. *Can I do this? Can I handle this?*

I spent a lot of time at the kitchen table where I did my readings, and that day I noticed unusual activity along the baseboards. Gizmo, my Maltese, was chasing what I thought was a dust bunny, but it turned out the creature was alive and had lots of feet . . . and lots of little friends. *Eeeek!* We had cockroaches!

Okay, I know I'm supposed to be all spiritual and loving, but let me tell you that if I'd had a flamethrower, I would have blasted all of 'em. I'd never had those things in any of my other homes, and I screamed and yelled for my friend Beth. We both took a look and found the bugs everywhere. I thought I was going to have a heart attack, I was so upset. Then it dawned on me. They were sending me an oracle message. They were letting me know by their own nature that not only would I survive, but I could call on their indestructible energy—this was a powerful message.

Great! Okay, got it. Now will you please go someplace else? Bugs in my house—even if they were sending me a message of hope and "hang in there, kid"—weren't my idea of fabulous. My friend, on the other hand, was a beautiful, gentle, sweet woman who would never hurt a flea (literally). If a creature was ever in need, Beth was sure to scoop it up and bring it home. I loved her for it, too. So that said, killing cockroaches was out of the question. You get the picture.

So here's where it gets really interesting. I'd read lots of fascinating books about the animistic or spiritualist view of the world. I was particularly struck that according to that worldview, everything had its own soul or spirit, and there was an oversoul that would look after a species. For example, the sacred sign of "eagle" comes from the spirit of all eagles and what they symbolize spiritually in the world. If we wanted to draw upon the symbolic power of eagle, we'd communicate with the "oversoul" of all eagles.

Based on this, I mustered a sort-of-confident tone and convinced Beth that we should have a little chat with the *über*spirit of the roaches. We actually had a good chuckle about this recently when I asked her permission to share the story. She reminded me that I presented my idea as if I talked to the oversouls of creatures all the time, and she just figured I knew what I was doing. The truth was that I'd never done any such thing and was just hoping with every bone in my body that it would work. But I was actually experiencing a big *Eeeew!*

Beth and I both prayed and meditated on the oversoul running the "cockroach universe," asking nicely if the bugs wouldn't mind going somewhere else. I explained that they were giving me anxiety, and although I was extremely grateful that they came to lend me their wonderful indestructible energy, I was going to be fine now. *I get your message; here are some crumbs; please eat up, suit up, and, er, move.*

The next day, the kitchen was completely devoid of the cockroach army. Not a single one could be found. We were both shocked by how fast they'd responded. It was amazing! I don't know why I was surprised, considering I do believe in these things, but I never cease to be astounded by how effortless it all is.

Beth and I never had a roach problem again. There was just a teeny side effect, however, as a result of our wonderful experience with interspecies communication. We heard a few days later that our next-door neighbor did get infested with our little friends. We didn't dare tell her why!

PART II

The Divine Dialogue

CHAPTER 5

WELCOME TO THE ONE-GOD CLUB

If we look at history, it's not hard to see that all deities have always been aspects of the One greatest unknowable Source, although humanity's beliefs have evolved over time. First we found the Divine in the natural world, then in multiple deities, and finally in One God, so it seems that ever since humans took their first breaths, everyone has been a member of the inclusive One-God Club, whether they've known it or not. In fact, this all-inclusive group allows every person an all-access pass to the wisdom of the Divine, when they ask for it.

As you read on, you'll come to understand what true membership in the One-God Club means and how to enjoy the benefits of your all-access pass. One of those benefits—the one I'm addressing in this book—is the way we can dialogue with the Divine through interactive oracles—signs and omens that appear in synchronicities, in other people, and in Nature. They speak to us through meaningful coincidences and answer our prayers via the sacred act of divination.

Messages from Spirit come to everyone. The challenge is committing to the inner work these transformative moments invite us to do. The mystical life, the active spiritual life, isn't an easy experience. It takes courage and fortitude to maintain and nurture the link between our mortal selves and our immortal consciousness by having an active relationship with God.

It's so easy to forget who we are and why we're here. It's no secret that the world is a challenging and soul-destroying place at times. And at some point, we realize that faith always needs to be an action rather than just a philosophical idea. We must *be* faith, not think faith. Let me explain.

We're spiritual beings learning through human experience. Messages from Spirit are meant to enhance this, to be mystical lights illuminating our paths. Yet it's important to know that they aren't going to do the work for us or give us the definitive answers to everything. Rather, they point to the right questions to ask. They guide us toward self-awareness and contemplation so that we can become more fully realized and authentic beings. Spirit messages can be warnings and can also provide clarity and inspiration—they may even show us details of the future. And so they can become an essential part of our experience of connecting to all that is part of the One.

Messages from Spirit are also an important entrance into the symbolic world of another kind of knowing. They maintain the bridge that shimmers between material reality and the mystery of the Great Unseen. Even with their inherent limitations . . . oracles, omens, and signs are magical doorways that allow a glimpse into the Light. Hopefully, seeing the Light will serve to wake us up and keep us conscious of our lifelong date with destiny and purpose. At the very least, we'll know that our presence in this life and in the greater cosmic plan really does matter.

So before embarking on a further exploration of the symbolic world—and since these ideas might still be new to you—I'd like to define some of the concepts you'll need to know and the terms I use to describe them. (I used many of these words and ideas through-out the first part of this book, where context provided meaning; but as you begin to examine your own life, it's important to clarify them.)

The Spirit in the Sky (and Everywhere Else)

I use the term *Spirit* to represent the essence of what we engage in Divine dialogue, or the sacred practice of divination. It signifies the complete wisdom and potential of the One God or Source, becoming known in the manifest world and in our personal experience. Spirit is the Divine living mirror in which we can inspect ourselves. We can see where we've come from, who we've become, and where we're heading on our journey.

There are many diverse words that you could use instead of *Spirit,* depending on your own belief system: the *I Am* Presence, the Sacred, Love, Light, Mind, Brahma, Nirvana, Cosmic Consciousness, the Great Unseen, All That Is, Infinite Higher Wisdom, or the Divine Matrix—or perhaps names used by science, such as the Field, the Quantum Field, the Submanifest Order of Being, or the Mind of Nature. Or you can use my personal favorite, which was coined by scientist and author Gary Schwartz: G.O.D., meaning Guiding-Organizing-Designing intelligence. These are just a few examples, and they're all interchangeable.

I choose *Spirit* because of its mystical, poetic, and fluid quality. I prefer the language of spirituality and mysticism because I feel that it captures the human experience as an expression of the soul in an evocative and meaningful way. I see the world as I believe it's meant to be seen—deep, complex, and rich with passion and meaning. Many years ago I heard someone say that "the All is in the small," and I've held on to that poetic idea because it expresses so simply what all of this is referring to.

I also like the word *Spirit* because it derives from the Latin root word *spirare,* which means "breath" or "to breathe." It's defined in the dictionary as the "vital principle or animating force within living beings." So imagine that God has breathed life into the Universe, leaving a Divine higher intelligence in everything. This breath of God, called Spirit, is what animates the material world and permeates the entire Great Unseen that surrounds us.

This intelligent force that's directly related to the mystery of God becomes the eternal wisdom available to everyone. We're all capable of reaching out into Spirit because we're created and animated by it. It keeps us connected to all of life; it shows us the details of our personal individual contracts where free will, fate, and destiny intersect.

For us to be aware of our Divine connection to all of Life through the medium of Spirit, we must awaken our consciousness and open our hearts and our capacity for compassion. And one of the ways in which we engage in this sacred conversation is through oracles.

Oracle Messages and Oracle Messengers

The word *oracle* comes from the Latin *oraculum,* rooted in the word *orare,* which means "to speak" or "to pray." Today, the dictionary defines *oracle* as "Divine message." Oracles can take one or all of three forms:

1. A person, whom I refer to as an *oracle messenger*

2. The message itself, which I refer to as an *oracle message*

3. A sacred object or tool used to interpret messages from Spirit interactively, which I refer to as *oracle tools* or *divination tools*

All of these are ways to engage in a dialogue with the Divine. Prayer and meditation are the actions required to begin the conversation.

Conversing with the Divine

The word *divination* refers to the act of contacting the soul world, the place where the infinite higher wisdom of the collective also resides in Spirit. It means simply talking to the Divine, asking for advice, and expecting an answer.

This conversation is conducted with special tools (which I'll discuss more in Part III), the substances or objects through which Spirit may be invited to speak and send messages. Using these tools to dialogue with the Infinite for guidance, confirmation, insight, solace, hope, and clarity—and the power to co-create a better world and find our authentic path—is meant to be a sacred act. It's about clarifying present circumstances in order to act rightly, and sometimes we can even reach into the future . . . if Spirit will show it to us.

We ask Spirit to reveal itself to us in mirror form. That way we can see ourselves reflected as we exist in the "eternal now," where past, present, and future are all one.

Divination is always an act of bridging the material and spiritual worlds in order to move from darkness into illumination. When using divination tools, seeking counsel from an oracle messenger, or looking for signs or omens, we're acknowledging and engaging the entire world, which has its own collective soul. We're recognizing the *anima mundi*—the world soul—as the true realm we live in.

Dr. Dianne Skafte's book *Listening to the Oracle,* one of the most comprehensive and thoughtful works on this subject, has a chapter entitled "Restoring Divination to the Divine," pointing to the rightful place of this art. Ancient thoughts support and inform the potential of our modern practice, and she reminds us that *divination* comes from the Latin word *divus,* which means "deity." "Therefore, to divine a thing is to discover the intention or the configuration of the Sacred in relation to that matter."

Divination is the act of engaging in a dialogue outside the mechanics and construct of the intellect and five senses, reaching out through *another knowing* to access wisdom beyond the personal self. It's all about moving outside of ordinary awareness to connect with the Divine. We allow the Source—called by whatever name we may choose—to become known through the manifest world. This practice engages the sixth sense, which is (in part) the capacity to access a higher awareness called *oracular consciousness.*

Oracular Consciousness

Oracular consciousness is inherent in every being on Earth. It's the pure, observant awareness that's always able to see beyond local reality. This transcends the confines of time and space and allows us to observe the mechanics of potential and possibility in the past-present-future space-time continuum. It's the part of us that can look at our experience from a nonlocal vantage point. That means our awareness or higher mind can see a bigger picture than our senses and present intellectual mind can measure in a "normal" way. Omens and signs are interpreted and experienced through this consciousness within all of us.

All of humanity knows the world from three different perspectives. Once you see that, it's easier to understand what, exactly, oracular consciousness taps into.

Sensory Reality

If you look through your physical eyes and your five senses, you can observe what exists in the material realm of "reality." I'm writing this while sitting in a chair on what I sense is solid, flat ground, with my dog Beanie cramming herself into the tiny space beside me. I know that there are 15 feet between me and the wall, which is upright and solid. I can smell the coffee beside me, and I can hear the clicking of the computer keys as I type. This is my local reality—"local" because it has a place in time and space. Why wouldn't I think that this is the sum total of what exists? In fact, many of us accept our perceived physical and measurable reality to be the only truth of what's "real." Why not believe that the earth is flat and the chair is solid?

Mind/Thinking Reality

Well, we don't think this planet is flat because we also observe the world through the mind. Science has now proven that Earth is round and everything is moving energy—not stable or solid at all. Science is the product of the mathematical thinking processes of the intellectual, analytical inner observer. The reason we know the world isn't flat is because of this mental capacity to observe and analyze "reality." Our senses say something different because only a particular type of observation is possible through them.

In the closing lecture at a Hay House I Can Do It!® conference, Deepak Chopra mentioned that science has concluded that the essential nature of the material world—the stuff of the universe— is actually "non-stuff." So is material reality what we believe it to be, or is it a product of our perception? We only see and observe a tiny portion of what's really there.

Both physical and mental "eyes" observe local reality. It has a location: Here is a book in your hands. The mind can conceive of nonlocal reality because it thinks. Yet where *are* your thoughts? Where are they stored? Do you have a giant locker somewhere marked "thoughts, memories, ideas"? If you open your skull, will someone be able to read the history of your thoughts inside it? What you're thinking doesn't exist in any known location, although you know that you're thinking in the now.

Stay with me here. This is where it gets interesting because you and I—here and now, in both local and nonlocal realities—are having a conversation in our minds. I'm having it with you in "my now"; you're having it with me in "your now." Our consciousness is connected, although we're in different moments in time and space. Our "nows" aren't happening at the same time, are they? I've left an imprint of my local reality and temporal consciousness for you to connect to at some other time—when you read this book. And I'm aware that you *will* be aware of my words.

You're now conscious of me. Where and when are we sharing this awareness? There's no known location in time and space except when you're actually having the experience. There's no physical spot for your awareness. Yet you're conscious, focused in the now, reading my words to you—hi there!

Soul/Awareness Reality

There's a consciousness behind your thinking mind, which is the *nonlocal* domain of Spirit. This is your soul, which is immortal, infinite, and eternal. It can't be confined and squashed into the little box that is temporarily "you." In other words, since you're a spiritual entity first, you're a nonlocal being who's "transiently local," as Deepak Chopra puts it. The soul is behind the person who's only here for a flash in the grand scheme of things.

Yet in the time that you're on Earth, it's possible to see through the soul's eyes and observe your life and all its potential from another point of view. You just get glimpses, though, because your purpose is to experience the world as a human being in a material universe, even if it's all an illusion.

The illusion itself is exciting because as you allow your awareness to expand and include those peeks delivered through oracular consciousness, you can experience many more facets of "reality" than you ever have before. Each layer you uncover breaks down the desperate need to control and define; it frees you to enjoy the true nature of uncertainty. Once you become conscious of the awareness behind your thoughts, all of what you consider to be reality shifts to include other perceptions. This is the domain of mystics and miracles, and of all paths that lead to the Light.

So the whole concept of oracular consciousness is engaging Spirit to manifest through the sensory/thinking reality. This provides evidence that Spirit does indeed exist everywhere and always. The ability to see ourselves in the mirror of Spirit is within us. Our intuition ignites the inner oracle.

Perhaps you'll gaze at clouds or oracle cards to see symbols that apply to your life, or receive a sign or omen either by synchronicity or in direct answer to a question. In every situation, oracular consciousness is the greater awareness that allows the Divine dialogue to begin and the answers to be given.

There's one caution I need to give you before you begin; and it concerns the possible ways you might misuse this exploration of oracles, omens, and signs.

Oracle Abuse

Why do you need to be watchful? Any method to engage the Light has a shadow that follows it. That shadow has nothing to do with "you-know-who" "down there," as is intimated by some. That's like saying "the devil made me do it," which is a big fat excuse for not taking responsibility for your own inherent flaws and darker leanings. The desire to know how things are going to turn out can become an obsession and treacherous, and then it's easy to lose sight of the most important experience—the now.

Human beings are unique in the fact that we're the only living beings on this planet who want to know what the future holds and control it at the same time. My dog doesn't stare at me and wonder if he'll have enough Milk-Bones in a couple years, or whether his yellow rubber-ducky squeaky toy will still be intact next week. He doesn't gaze out of the window, wondering if I'll be able to pay the mortgage on our house. Nor does he come to me, wagging his tail, concerned that I may have too many tour dates next year. The main point is that other sentient beings exist fully in the now—and their lives have no less value than ours, and perhaps a whole lot more freedom.

We're choice makers and intellectual creatures, gifted with the knowledge of our mortality and burdened with the existential fear of death that remains in our psyche from the moment we recognize it. Trapped in a bubble marked "Me," we spend our lives making sure we're safe, fed, loved, and getting what we desire and need. We don't wish to suffer, and we want all that we can get.

There's nothing wrong with any of this, and connecting to Spirit will only enhance and expand our personal and collective experience. It's when we become crazed by needing to know everything in advance, or we look to the world for signs at the expense of making rational choices and decisions, that the dialogue loses its Divine nature and becomes a shadowy, destructive force. The point of engaging oracular consciousness—the inherent "other knowing" within us that connects to Spirit—is to be empowered. We become disempowered when we abuse it by overuse.

I know this from experience. I developed a policy of allowing clients access to my service a maximum of twice a year because I ran into many people who were addicted to going to psychics. My own capacity to See for them was diluted, given that I was reading signs of obsession, not dealing with someone who had the relative detachment essential for a good reading. These individuals were suffering from their compulsion to know a specific outcome, especially the one they wanted. Given that the oracle messenger and the person querying are always a team, the readings lost their potential spiritual value and impact.

For example, let's say Jane wants to know if her alcoholic, married boyfriend will leave his wife for her. She goes to nine different intuitives or psychics wanting to hear that he will—any day now. Jane isn't interested in an oracle telling her that this pattern of obsessing over unavailable men is harming her and that she needs to address her attraction to a practicing alcoholic in order to have a healthy life. She doesn't want to hear that her happiness will come only when she surrenders and asks how to heal. She certainly doesn't want to know that she's made this situation her Higher Power and given body, mind, and soul to it. And she doesn't want to be told that she's cut off spiritually. She'll spend a fortune going from oracle to oracle, hoping that she'll hear what she wants—which is unlikely to happen.

In fact, oracle messengers themselves—if they're not astute enough to recognize the energy or how Spirit is using them—may see the desired outcome, which will actually be wrong. Both oracle messenger and recipient become part of a curious and destructive involuntary dance. I know because I've been on both sides. I've been humbled this way by insisting that the future be open to me when it wasn't meant to be. This is a reminder that Spirit is always in charge, not me.

There's an interesting phenomenon that arises here, actually. Oracles, omens, and signs are just mirrors of what already exists. Your energy is reflected in them. So if you're crazed and obsessive, you'll get crazed and obsessive signs to remain that way until you bottom out. Oracles then act as catalysts, forcing you down the same path over and over until you can't take it anymore. It's the hard way to learn, but until you do so, the patterns are doomed to repeat.

Oracles then pose as tricksters, reflecting the deep denial you may have about the truth. This is when they appear unrelenting, mercilessly disempowering both sides of the dialogue. In fact, when these oracles seem false, they're only reflecting the shadow you refuse to acknowledge. This is one of the reasons why I advocate approaching the dialogue with sincerity and detachment, lest you get caught in the mire of the ego's false sense of control and neediness.

The same thing happens if you use divination tools too often, compulsively throwing oracle cards, swinging a pendulum, adding numbers, or misinterpreting signs because of emotional attachment. This goes against the intuitive voice of your own oracular consciousness, and the dependency can become devastating. You can really get lost, missing the truth in the shadows of your motivation.

Since desire just creates more desire, we have to be cautious and allow our curiosity to be led by a higher impulse than just wanting to know that our wishes will be fulfilled. The good news is that oracle abuse is easy to spot, and once it's run its course we'll hopefully know not to do it again. Only false power beckons from the shadows of oracles, and no good comes until the experience forces self-evaluation. Only then does oracle abuse lead to spiritual sobriety.

Another important point to consider is that sometimes we aren't meant to know something in advance. We might be encouraged to learn something through an unpleasant experience. That's the way things go sometimes. Fate and destiny are meant to play out as they will. All of us participate in "stories" where temporary blindness may be necessary for our growth.

"If it be Thy will" should be the statement at the end of every prayer and before asking for a sign, visiting an oracle messenger, using divination to connect to Spirit, or requesting guidance. We need to remember that we may be faced with riddles and questions instead of direct answers because we're supposed to do more of the work ourselves. Spirit decides what we're meant to know and if it's for our highest good. Sometimes we ask about a particular situation but receive guidance about something else that's more important.

Once you make conscious contact, Spirit also decides exactly what the conversation is going to be about. A good question is: *What should I know today to help my authentic service?* This allows the pertinent aspects of your life to be illuminated and examined.

Predictions, Potentials, and the Power of Now

It's true that the future can be seen at times, but there can be no guarantees that you'll get to view it the way it will really be. Such vision is a paradoxical gift, because your relationship to the future is active, not passive. If you see something positive, then the question is: *What right action will help me keep on course?* When something challenging or difficult is revealed, you can ask: *What, if anything, can I do to change this?*

More often, an oracle message or prediction speaks to the potential or probability of a situation, especially if the elements can be affected by choice. No oracle will consistently give us absolute access to the future. It's in the "now" that we have the greatest power to progress; and by understanding the past, we see how our patterns began. How we perceive ourselves and the clarity of our intentions change the outcome of future events. Oracles, omens, and signs are most powerful when they're used to illuminate the present, for all events must flow from the point where we can be transformed.

Profound change and self-revelation in the powerful now can alter the course of events. This happens as you become aware and awake. If you focus your query on how to become more authentic and prosperous or on how to heal your inner wounds, you automatically have a greater chance to glimpse a more abundant and peaceful experience, which in turn influences everything that is to come.

When you ask about the future and it's made available for you to see, simply regard that as encouragement to continue with the steps needed to get there. Encouragement is a good thing, but the days to come are never guaranteed. Seeing the future doesn't change the moment you're in—you still need to live in each second until you arrive. Staring longingly at the destination doesn't help you get there quicker, anyway.

So tread lightly when asking for the future to be revealed, because that may not be what's needed or even valuable for you. With reverence, humility, and clarity of intention, you can step forward with peace in your heart, knowing that you're asking with higher purpose.

This story from one of my clients shows how an oracle message illuminated the now, and how she persisted in not wanting to hear it.

A Lesson from a Repeated Oracle Card

I used to work for a nonprofit organization that was going through some serious identity issues. This resulted in the staff feeling negative and being treated really poorly. People could feel the heaviness whenever they walked into the office. I believed things would sort themselves out, so I stayed there. I didn't want those who were more vulnerable than I was to suffer, as I thought they would without me standing up for them. The lesson of this situation was a hard one to learn, but it kept beating at my door.

I'd just started using oracle cards and was doing a self-reading at least once a night over a period of about three months, searching for answers about my situation and those at the office. What should I do? How could I improve the situation? Why was everything so horrible? When would it get better? There was one card that seemed to fly out of the deck over and over and that kept coming up in my readings. It always made me cry, although I didn't understand why at the time. I just got frustrated when it would appear again and again. One night, I even took it out of the deck before beginning my reading. The picture on the card was of a woman embracing herself.

Looking back, I know exactly why it kept appearing. I was convinced that the answer to the toxic situation lay in helping others, but I was clearly being guided to start taking care of myself.

I knew that my questions were always answered, but that didn't mean I listened. I'd become so unbalanced, and Spirit was asking me to honor my own needs, which included leaving that job. I wasn't responsible for those who chose to stay, and I was doing no one any good by remaining in such a negative environment. To this day, I remember that experience with both amazement (that I stayed as long as I did) and gratitude for the important lesson I learned. To honor oneself is to honor all. I also pay extra-special attention these days to any oracle cards that continue to appear. The card that searched me out during that time very rarely shows up in my readings now.

Signs May Not Mean What You Think They Mean

Knowing the future—just standing on its own, divested from its relationship to surrounding events—can actually be confusing. I think Spirit throws us a curveball sometimes just to keep us a bit off balance and to teach us a lesson! Or sometimes what appears to be deep is shallow, and we end up saying, "Huh?" We have to be careful not to read too much into things or notice only what we want to see when we do make a connection to Spirit. Signs may seem like they mean one thing in the moment, but later on their true significance will be revealed. This is especially true when the Divine makes a connection to us spontaneously. One thing is for certain, though—Spirit is communicating with us all the time. That is a profound sign in itself.

Just remember as you journey through this book that the more you dialogue with Spirit and receive its messages, becoming more awake and alert, the more you'll know that loving-kindness is the key to all action. *In Spirit we belong; in Spirit we are One.*

So how do we get around all the superstitious stuff about oracles, omens, and signs? Read on and explore some more.

CHAPTER 6

LANGUAGE, LABELS, AND LIMITATIONS

I had a very disturbing yet enlightening conversation with a radio interviewer a few months after my first book, *Remembering the Future,* was released. Normally, the people interested in talking to me were aware of the content of my book, but this man admitted that he didn't know anything about it until the night before my interview. He opened his comments to me in an aggressive yet well-spoken and polite manner, citing his difficulty with the fact that in my book I mentioned psychic Sylvia Browne and theologian Thomas More "in the same breath." He went through my bibliography, letting me know that he agreed with some of the references but was highly suspicious of others. He was supportive of the gift of prophecy, but not visions or information gathered by a psychic. *And the difference is?* I wondered. There isn't any, actually. It's all about words.

He wanted to know why I wasn't calling myself a prophet since prophets receive their visions from God. And in the same statement, he implied that psychics get their information from "the guy down there." *Right—here we go again with the red guy with horns and fire.*

At that point I was looking around for cameras in my house to see if I was on an episode of *New Age Punk'd!* The radio host told me that his confusion deepened (as did mine—immensely) because in my book I identified myself as a Christian. How could that be, he wanted to know, when I encouraged people to empty their minds through meditation? In his estimation, this was akin to inviting the evil guy with horns to come on in and mess with people's minds. I was really surprised, and at first I thought he was kidding—especially when he asked me if I was afraid of demons entering a person through meditation or divination. *Yikes!*

True, I do call the wounded ego an "inner Goblin" as a metaphor for how we can sabotage ourselves. But a real live demon coming from "you know where" isn't part of my line of thinking or experience at all.

"Biblical demons? You've *got* to be kidding!"

He was dead serious.

The interview really freaked me out because I was shocked and unprepared for a conversation like that. I didn't know quite how to respond to it. I was equally fascinated and repelled by his adamant vision of a world in need of protection from the evil horned bad guy who was hiding somewhere in the New Age community, ready to snag believers while they meditated. Yet I knew he was sincere in his views. After I respectfully hung up, I knew that I had to do some serious studying, so I decided to look back at history to find out why there's so much prejudice and superstition about the paranormal. When and where did this all begin? I started with some research on the word *demon,* and lo and behold, I found some fascinating information with respect to the language used to describe divination, oracles, omens, and signs.

From Daemon to Demon

The victors are always the ones who write history books. It's never the losers, never the victims. We see this most clearly with the turbulent and sometimes violent rise of monotheism when the God of Abraham took the place of the many gods of antiquity.

As one culture evolved into another, a convenient phenomenon occurred: The deities of the older society all became minions of evil. In other words, the old gods became the new demons. Rather than trying to understand them or considering the possibility that the gods were, in fact, many aspects of the One, it was a lot easier to wipe them out and start all over again. After all, everybody knows that "our way is the right way."

In this process, we can see how easily the so-called evidence appeared, showing that evil had existed everywhere until the arrival of the only true God. Well, we're all saved now, right? Everything that came before was declared to be without value, basically obliterating the mark of any other group on cultural evolution. What was once sacred became marked as profane. Period.

Let's take Gnosticism and the pagan mysteries as examples. They predated Christianity as spiritual traditions in which *gnosis* was the goal. Gnostics sought a direct personal experience of the Divine, as opposed to just having faith. Personal mystical revelation was achieved without a priest as an intermediary between the person and the Sacred.

The *daemon* was the name for one of two parts of a human's dualistic nature—it represented the higher self; the lower self was called the *eidolon*. In their book *The Jesus Mysteries,* authors Timothy Freke and Peter Gandy observe:

> The Pagan sages taught that every human being has a mortal lower self called the *eidolon* and an immortal Higher Self called the *Daemon.* The eidolon is the embodied self, the physical body, and personality. The Daemon is the Spirit, the true Self, which is each person's spiritual connection to God. The Mysteries were designed to help initiates realize that the eidolon is a false self and that their true identity is the immortal Daemon. . . .
>
> Although it appears as if each person has their own Daemon or Higher Self, the enlightened initiate discovers that actually there is one Daemon shared by all—a universal Self, which inhabits every being. Each soul is a part of the one Soul of God. To know oneself therefore is to know God.

These mystical teachings are found both in the Pagan Mysteries and Gnostic Christianity.

The daemon was another name for the immortal soul. When approaching Divine dialogue through divination, it's this higher self (or daemon) that engages in dialogue with the Source. According to the old language, you're engaging the daemon to reach into Spirit for enlightenment, reflection, and revelation.

Since daemonic reality represented the otherworld, where you search for the essence of the wisdom of the Divine as opposed to the mortal material world, you can see how this is going to go. Spirit was regarded as the daemonic reality—the soul world of the higher self that transcends the earthbound ego. It was also the domain of the universal self that's the collective intermediary between humans and God. It allowed the Divine intelligence and wisdom to send us messages and dialogue with us through interactive divination tools, oracles, signs, and omens (which were sent to us through the natural world).

So what happened to the daemon of the pagans and Gnostics? The concept of daemon and eidolon didn't serve the new replacement faith. With the advent of patriarchy and the systematic obliteration of any theology that allowed individual access to the Divine, *daemon* became the *demon,* an evil trickster that would surely lead people away from God. This conversion had grave consequences: The personal and universal connector to Spirit, as described by the pagans and Gnostics, became something evil and untrustworthy. Everything changed.

After rewriting the old ways, how about we take what's left; shred it; put it in a pot; and add a cup of fear, a pinch of ignorance, and a spoonful of superstition. Then stir it up and watch it go the way of the blasphemous heathens. "Double, double, toil and trouble"; I smell a witch burning! The *daemon,* our personal connector to God, conveniently becomes the *demon* of the devil.

You can see how powerful language is. Just by removing the letter *a* from the word, something very different is born—something that suits the new way of connecting with God.

Also, way back in history, there was a belief that destructive and evil beings called demons actually existed, residing somewhere in the unseen and spending their time making serious messes for us poor unsuspecting human victims. It was convenient to believe that an oracle was communicating with those creatures, especially if you were afraid of the oracle's power to reveal things you'd prefer to be kept hidden. These beliefs are still held by many people today, although none of the folks I asked knew why they think these things: "I just do. Also, somewhere in the Bible it says so." Lots more research ahead for me.

So in fact, my radio interviewer was taught that divination and engaging the sixth sense had something to do with demons. I get it now. I can't really fault him for bringing up demons, as he was taught about them, and it wasn't by accident.

However, the next time somebody mentions the subject, I'll say, "Yes, indeed! But it's a *daemon*, honey! Just don't forget the *a.* Oh, and pass the eye of newt . . . and some fried bat wings would be nice, too. Yum."

Beauty and Unity in Diversity

At this juncture, I'd like to say that I appreciate that you'll have your own beliefs, and I have no desire to disrespect them. This is a topic with a big electric charge, but it bears discussing, given the nature of this book.

Although I was raised as a Christian and find much of the religion beautiful, I also have a deep reverence for many other sacred spiritual traditions. I've always been fascinated by humankind's history of finding different relationships with the Light. Divination and receiving Divine guidance from oracles, omens, and signs is acceptable in some forms of religious expression, and heretical in others. We can run into problems when we start saying: "You show me yours, and I'll show you mine" or "My way is the only way," instead of identifying with the common Spirit behind it all. We need to remember that everyone is just asking for guidance from the Divine. The question is how we can identify the common essence rather than compare the diverse forms.

Lost in Translations and Transitions

We need to remember that all religions and sacred spiritual traditions developed as an answer to our eternal need to understand our human relationship with the great Mystery. They've evolved as we have. They all borrow from the past and frequently replace one tradition with similar practices and new versions of myths, which are more relevant to the prevailing sociopolitical climate. Consider the Egyptian myth of the sun god Horus that Christ resembles.

My point is to show how certain truths get lost in the transition, and certainly in translation. Even the god Yahweh was anthropomorphized and plucked out of relative obscurity to become the representative of the God behind all gods (if you will). My point in bringing up all of this is to illustrate how the sacred practice of divination and exploring the world of oracles, omens, and signs was lost during the emergence of the centralized, monotheistic patriarchy. This goes for all three religions—Judaism, Christianity, and Islam—coming from the "One God."

In Gregg Braden's book *The God Code,* he explains that the DNA code in all carbon-based life, specifically us humans, spells YHVH in the ancient language of Aramaic. This literally means "God/Eternal within the body." If that's true, all of us should have access to Spirit. After all, it's the breath of God that gives us life and is everywhere. Here, our experience is recognized as part of a vast system in which we're all connected, instead of the divisions encouraged by religious belief.

Although the impulse to have a relationship with Spirit has been the same since time immemorial, we can always find ways to differ. For example, I have a personal teensy-weensy issue about the traditional concept of heaven and hell. In my opinion that's a throwback to the ancient idea that the universe was a sandwich, with humans in the important middle part; heaven above, where all the good people go to play harps and be happy just staring at God; and hell below, where all the bad folks end up burning in fire pits, listening to screaming heavy-metal music! Granted, that was the accepted view when everybody believed the earth was flat. (Although heavy-metal music was something I just threw in, since all those music videos look like hell.) I also don't believe in the devil as an evil red guy with horns who lives "down there," and I'm not particularly interested in any demons or dark forces, either.

I feel the same way about the idea that God is a testy, old white man in the sky, doling out punishments or prizes. It's my belief that God is light, life, love, and the ultimate consciousness of the creative force in the Universe—but you don't have to believe this. I also know that there's a feminine face of God to complete the picture, but that is, again, simply another form that allows me to experience or express my connection to what is always a Mystery.

When someone implies that my service as an intuitive is devil's work and that engaging in divination as a form of Divine dialogue is about communing with demons, I'm completely baffled. Loving God, asking for guidance to serve and do only good works, helping others develop conscious contact with the Divine, encouraging faith, respecting all of Life, and helping people wisely choose the path of the greatest good aren't part of the general job description of Blasphemous Devil's Minion. At least, not last time I checked.

So now that the devil's out of the way, let's talk some more about words and labels and how they can cause as much trouble today as they did a couple thousand years ago. Take the word *divination*. It tends to stir up all kinds of confusion and superstition, encouraged by some religions' misunderstanding of it.

So let's look at how all of this works and how the contradictory religious decision of banning divination practices came about. I think it's worthwhile to educate ourselves on all the aspects of a practice, especially one that has such a rich history.

Location, Location, Location

If Spirit is everywhere—in and around every living thing—then the One God is immanently within *us*. This directly challenges the idea that God is a supernatural old white man located way up in the sky. It can also raise difficulties for someone who believes that God and heaven are physically located somewhere above, hell is below, and we're in the middle waiting to go to either place. Some people consider it blasphemous to suggest anything else.

We humans need to place things in time and space, since we typically perceive everything through our five senses and rational, intellectual minds. It's important to understand this when we venture into exploring messages from Spirit through oracles, omens, and signs, since they don't always follow those temporal and spatial guidelines—especially when the future or details of the past are revealed in a reading.

To some, oracles, interpreting omens and signs, and using divination as a means for direct contact with the Divine are sins. Although the traditional idea of a "transgression against God" is mentioned in the dictionary, one of the meanings of the word *sin* is "a vitiated state of human nature in which the self is estranged from God." I had to look up the word *vitiate,* which means "to make ineffective." So this definition really appealed to me, as I believe our greatest error is to perceive ourselves separated from God and from one another, which essentially makes us completely ineffective in co-creating with the Divine. And that, after all, is why we're here.

Remember, we exist as individuated sparks of the Divine so that It/He/She can be expressed through us. Divination's sole purpose is to perceive and know the Divine made manifest. If we understand that Spirit is the intelligent source energy of the Divine, and the source of the information relayed in the dialogue, divination can actually be seen as a way to rectify the estrangement of "sin."

The term *manifest* is a catchy word that's used loosely and frequently these days. It comes from an interesting Latin term: *manifestus,* which means "caught in the act." So we're really looking to catch Spirit in the act of showing up in our lives, much like the child who finds Santa Claus eating cookies and drinking milk in front of the wonderful gifts under the tree. The difference is that we do actually get to see Spirit if we learn to pay attention to our intuitive experiences. We receive Divine messages through oracles, omens, signs, and other forms in which Spirit manifests throughout our world.

Misinterpretations and Misunderstandings

Let me say here that I'm no theologian, nor do I claim to be an expert on religious texts. I started digging around to find out why divination, psychics, astrologers, mediums, and the like were banned. I wanted to discover why some people still believe this nonsense about it all being under the jurisdiction of evil.

Here's what I found: Divination became an outlawed form of Divine dialogue only according to the three religions that formed under the God of Abraham—Judaism, Christianity, and Islam. What's most pertinent and interesting is a misinterpreted biblical passage that's the favorite one quoted by those people today who've been taught that divinatory practices are a sin—as well as the Inquisitors of old. In essence, the authors of these parts of Deuteronomy claimed that God decreed that divination was to be banned, along with fortune-telling, channeling, sorcery, astrology, seers, necromancy, wizardry, magic, and other practices mostly attributed to the older pagan cultures being wiped out at that time.

According to many Bible scholars, the real motivation for banning divination practices was that only the One God was to be consulted rather than the many deities that were henceforth deemed false idols. Remember that the One True God of Abraham was Yahweh, who originated as a god among many gods worshipped at that time. Abraham's God (the same One who's present in our current monotheistic religions) supplanted all the others at a key moment in history. In rejecting the worship of the golden calf and other idols and declaring Yahweh the One True God, all sacred practices relating to communicating with any other deity but Yahweh were rendered illegal. There was now only supposed to be the One.

Remember as well that up until this time, the spiritual traditions of the people were oral, not written. When these laws were written down, they were translations and interpretations of what was believed to be known and accepted. But how can we really know the authenticity of their content?

Another interesting point to keep in mind is this: The scrolls that were said to have been found and enforced—literally to the letter—by the Deuteronomists, were declared to have content that was dictated at that time to Moses by Yahweh Himself. But according to Karen Armstrong in her book *The Great Transformation*, scholars now think that these stories and laws were written down long after they'd first been expressed orally.

In any event, at that point there was a written text of what's believed to be holy law, and it was new for the people of the time. Thus began the banning of sacred divination practices and the consequent mass declaration of their "demonic roots." It started as a political way to centralize worship around the God Yahweh. This was only the beginning, however, as the worship of Yahweh wasn't the predominant religion at the time.

What also seems to be at the root of the prejudice against most messages from Spirit was that divination allowed an individual personal access to Divine guidance. This was politically and economically threatening to the Roman church, which finally—1,000 years later—sanctioned those ancient interpretations and all the other pertinent content that went into what became the Holy Bible at the Nicene Council in A.D. 325. So it was at that point in history, at the advent of Christianity, when any personal direct practice of Divine dialogue was banned.

The real purpose at the beginning of the new Roman Christian religion was to keep the people dependent on the church and its centralized power structure of the pope and a hierarchy of clergy. And the people were, indeed, made wholly dependent on this institution. The church wanted souls and, most important, money. People had to pay for absolution and blessings, and Divine guidance was only to be had from a priest. The accepted and enforced edict against divination and other oracular practices (including ancient healing methods) was, and still is, interpreted by some as long-standing moral law. This is hardly accurate, as even the apostles used divination when they cast lots. In my opinion, it was really a law of economics, power, and politics.

It seems that religious prejudice against divinatory practices and oracles, and the interpreting of signs and omens, also came from having unclear boundaries about whose job it was to declare what came from God and what didn't. Questions arose not only about the content of messages, but also—and more important— which God they came from. Well, only the newest version of God was the Truth. When it comes to some religious opinions, the same applies today.

So if a practice arises from another culture or from a sacred tradition that's already been displaced, it unfortunately gets to be deemed false or evil. As I mentioned, look closely at many organized religions and you'll find that they've tended to plagiarize slightly and borrow from each other as they replaced one tradition with similar, newer versions. Nevertheless, the old gods must be demons or worse—manifestations of the "big bad you-know-who down there" himself.

Another justification for this prejudice is that God alone endorses the experience of prophecy through oracles, omens, signs, and dreams that have been deemed acceptable—or so we're told. But who gets to say?

Aren't all gods manifestations of our need to explain the Divine as the inherent higher intelligence behind what we see? The gods may have changed from the many to the One, but Spirit—the living breath, essence, and wisdom of the truly unknowable God— remains constant.

The Bible and Divination

In the Bible, God tells the childless Abraham that he'll be the father of many nations. How is he told? Clearly he's accessing an inner knowing or higher sense that resides in the part of him that's Divine. Is this not the place from which all knowing arises, and is this not a gift from the Creator? Jesus goes into the desert for 40 days to pray and fast. There he's tempted by the "devil." In India, the Hindu ascetic sannyasis have a similar practice, where they renounce the world and explore the self to confront the individual "shadow." There are numerous similarities throughout the sacred traditions of many other cultures.

So in the end, aren't we all saying the same thing? It's only perspective that changes and distorts. There would be no Bible without the presence of oracle and oracular consciousness, for without it no one would be able to interpret the awesome language of God. It's unknowable unless we can put aside encumbered thoughts and enter the world of symbols and signs.

The Bible itself (as is the case with most sacred religious traditions, both oral and written) is essentially based on prophetic visions, dreams, and the interpretation of signs from God. In fact, there are hundreds of cases supporting and even encouraging the practice of divination and prophecy throughout the Bible, in both the Old and New Testaments.

There's tons of evidence that divination was used for Divine guidance by very important figures in religious history that followed the One God of Abraham. Moses consulted Spirit by using a tool that was revealed to him by God. He had a vision that led him to create the Urim and Thummim. This is known as the highest divination tool in the Bible, and it was consulted as a sacred tool by the Jews (which is described in Exodus).

In the Old Testament, the word *oracle* is used to denote the most holy place in the temple in every case but one. The exception is in the book of Samuel, where it means "the word of God." A man inquired "at the oracle of God" by means of the Urim and Thummim in the breastplate on the high priest's ephod (or vestment). In the New Testament, the word *oracle* is used only in the plural and always denotes the word of God. The scriptures are called *living oracles* because of their power to transform.

Divination as a means of connecting with the Divine is evidenced throughout the rest of the Bible, where countless stories mention and even encourage it. Here are some examples of what the Bible says about oracles and receiving messages from Spirit:

1 Corinthians 14:3: *But everyone who prophesies speaks to men for their strengthening, encouragement and comfort.*

1 Corinthians 14:29, 31–33: *Two or three prophets should speak, and the others should weigh carefully what is said. . . . For you can all prophesy in turn so that everyone may be instructed and encouraged. The spirits of prophets are subject to the control of prophets. For God is not a God of disorder but of peace.*

1 Corinthians 14:36–38: *Did the word of God originate with you? Or are you the only people it has reached? If anybody thinks he is a prophet or spiritually gifted, let him acknowledge that what I am writing to you is the Lord's command. If he ignores this, he himself will be ignored.*

Joel 2:28–30: *". . . I will pour out my Spirit on all people. Your sons and daughters will prophesy, your old men will dream dreams, your young men will see visions. Even on my servants, both men and women, I will pour out my Spirit in those days. I will show wonders in the heavens and on the earth . . ."*

As another example, Ezekiel was a priest by training and a prophet by God's call, who received vivid visions and delivered powerful messages. God uses people through whom he can work. There's no exclusive club consisting of an elite group of people who can make contact with the Divine and receive a message. Won't we receive an answer if we're asking: *What is the highest good? What is God's will?* Messages from Spirit are for everyone seeking guidance on the path to goodness, regardless of religious affiliation.

The Common Threads of Gold
in the Human Spiritual Tapestry

We live in turbulent times, and fear is instilled in us everywhere we turn. But when hasn't it been like this? The only difference now is that we have more ways to destroy each other and the planet, and terror can be advertised on the news. This is a global experience these days, not a local one. As long as human beings roam the planet and behave badly, there will be no peace. But that can change!

Humanity appears to be divided because of religious beliefs and ethnicity. But for all our differences based on skin color and metaphysical assumptions, where many claim the exclusive status of "chosen by God," there exists a uniting thread of beauty. It's impossible to convince every human being to believe in the same version of God. Yet common to all sacred texts is one strong, golden thread.

In order for us to achieve the goals that we long for—peace, shelter, food, safety, community, and love—we can come together in the Golden Rule. This one thread that's been woven into the core of all true spiritual pursuits reminds us of the most powerful idea of all: It's not what we believe dogmatically that's important, but ultimately how we behave toward each other and all sentient life. This Golden Rule is also known as the Law of Kindness. This is the intention behind the dialogue between us and the Divine, when we look to oracles, omens, and signs for guidance. This is the basis for the statement "for the highest good of all" when we're asking Spirit for a sign to point us toward the next right action. We need to be kind, and we need to have faith in God.

"Do unto others as you would have them do unto you . . ."
— Matthew 7:12, Christian text

"As a man sows so shall he reap."
— Galatians 6:7, Christian text

"Treat others as you would be treated. What you like not for yourself dispense not to others."
— Abdullah Ansari, from an Islamic Sufi text

"Hurt not others with that which pains you yourself."
— Udanavarga, Buddhist text

"What is hateful to thee, do not unto thy fellow."
— Rabbi Hillel, from the Talmud

"Do not unto others what you would not they should do unto you."
— Analects, Confucian text

"This is the sum of duty: Do nothing unto others which, if done to you would cause you pain."
— Mahabharata, Hindu text

"A man should wander about treating all creatures as he himself would be treated."
— Sutrakritanga, Jain text

Spirit knows no differences between us. We're all the same in Spirit; and in the community of Spirit, we're one. Even if our beliefs differ and our fundamental views on God—and how we serve that God—are polarized, this is where we can come together and how we find our sacred places in life's dance. This concept of unity in diversity can be a powerful reunion of us all.

I heard a story that I believe is attributed to a Hopi legend that provides an image for this idea. Imagine that all religions that have ever existed have at their core a golden thread that reaches up to God. Alone, they may be beautiful, but they're not strong enough to hold the weight of everyone. Alone, the threads are thin and weak because they're separate.

Then imagine weaving all the threads together, gently and respectfully, to form a rope. The rope is incredibly strong, with each individual thread exactly in the right place. This creates the strength to hold the weight of all peoples. With this rope, all of humanity can reach God. Everyone can climb and find the highest purpose for all of Life. All of us—regardless of color, race, or creed—can reach the Divine.

Oracles, omens, and signs are reminders that Spirit is listening, watching, and forever reflecting our climb toward what is highest within us. It's helping us heal the things we hide in the darkest parts of our shadows. The Golden Rule is the common thread that becomes the strong rope. This is how we need to behave so that messages from Spirit can transform us and restore what's been lost in the world.

Intention Is Everything

What's most important here isn't that we all agree on some religion's take on a personal dialogue with the Divine. The key is the deeper spiritual Mystery that all of us are involved in, regardless of creed. It's important now to agree on the modern intention of divination rather than argue its history.

All oracles are neutral until they're used to relay a message. Mrs. Kelly was just my nanny until she saw visions dancing for me above the cards. When the oracle at Delphi was eating her lunch and not on her stool talking to the king of Sparta, she wasn't anything but a woman in a nice toga with spinach in her teeth. An oracle message written on a piece of paper for Sue won't mean anything to Mary, and if nobody reads it . . . it doesn't mean anything at all.

Divination tools—or interactive oracles—are also neutral. They range from simple objects like pendulums to the elements of complicated systems, such as the coins or yarrow sticks of the *I Ching,* or *Book of Changes,* and the cards of the tarot. They derive their language from the movements of the stars and the numbers of sacred geometry. They're found in the patterns of coffee grounds or tea leaves. Although designated for sacred purposes, the objects or systems sit there without power until you have the intention to use them. Without intention, coffee grounds on the bottom of a cup are just destined for the dishwasher.

Here's a simple example. A telephone sitting on a table is just a human-made communication device. Until you pick it up, it's completely neutral. If you make a call to your mom to tell her that you love her, it becomes a wonderful bridge between you. It's activated by your picking it up and dialing a number, and then it's given meaning by what you convey. If you use it for work, for example, it becomes a tool for productivity. It can be seen as positive when the intention in using it is positive.

The same telephone can be picked up and used to plan a robbery. Or you can dial people and insult them or say something dishonest. If the intention is to harm someone, then the communication tool can be a bridge of negativity.

A knife sitting on a counter is just a sharp piece of metal in a wooden handle. It can be used to chop vegetables, or it can be used to kill someone. The knife itself was created as a tool to cut, but it's given active power only when used with intention.

A star in the sky just twinkles prettily in the night until you see its astrological significance in relationship to an event or a person. An animal in the forest appears just as another creature until its presence is acknowledged in a higher context representing a synchronistic message from Spirit.

So when using interactive divination tools and observing a dialogue with the Sacred, our intention must always be for the highest Truth. We seek knowledge to sustain life and to be co-creative with the Divine. It's always about the Light, never the dark—although the Light may, in fact, illuminate a shadow. In that case, the darker elements can be brought forward to be cleansed, healed, and released.

In this way, we can explore without fear—and with confidence that with right intention and faith we may seek guidance from Spirit and the All That Is and receive it with grace and humility. Messages from Spirit come from the Light, and in this book, those are the only ones we're interested in.

So read on now, and explore.

CHAPTER 7

THE COMMON CLEDON

Before you learn some of the fun and interesting ways to start the conversation with Spirit, there's one spontaneous form of oracle message that you should know about. As I mentioned earlier, it's called the *Cledon,* and it works in a very specific way. It's a message from Spirit that's innocently and unknowingly delivered to you by someone. Once you've asked for a message from Spirit, go out into the world and listen. Perhaps a stranger in conversation with a friend will say the exact words you needed to hear—and the person may not even notice you. Or you might turn on the radio and hear a song that speaks to your exact situation. This is the kind of Cledon that Spirit delivers to you spontaneously, which will serve as Divine guidance.

As a matter of fact, way back in ancient Rome, it was an accepted practice to pray to the gods for an answer to a particular issue and then go out into the world and eavesdrop on other people's conversations to hear an answer. This was an expected way for Spirit to deliver a message.

When I started my first Hay House tour, providing live readings in front of very large groups of people, this phenomenon began to occur regularly. I was invariably approached by more than one person after each event, letting me know they were sure that when I'd been talking to the individual in front of me, I'd also been delivering a message to *them*. Some were absolutely sure and insisted on giving me all the details; others were confused but hopeful because what they felt and experienced had been so personally compelling.

For example, say I connected to Mary's deceased father, John, who drove a dark blue truck with a dent in its right side. He'd died in a boating accident, and his second wife's name was Joan. Could I not also have been unknowingly receiving a message for an audience member named Joan, whose mother's name was Mary and whose father, John, had also driven a dented dark blue truck and died in a boating accident? She might truly believe I was also talking to her. Further, could I also be telling Joan—as well as Mary— that the father who was so abusive in this life wanted forgiveness and wished to make amends? Both women can be convinced that the message was equally personal and meaningful.

I also get letters and e-mails from listeners after my weekly radio show, thanking me for being the messenger for them even when I'd been talking to someone else. For them, I am the conduit for intimate advice, and they want to share its impact with me.

This has been my experience over and over again, and after a while it began to intrigue me. Looking back over the years, I realized that I, too, have been the recipient of similar synchronistic moments, listening to words spoken by others not logically directed to me, but with deep and meaningful spiritual impact.

In my early days of recovery from alcoholism and drug addiction, 20-plus years ago, I attended group meetings with other recovering people and listened to them share their personal experiences. More often than not, it seemed like they were directing their words to me, but that clearly wasn't the case. I could identify so strongly with what I heard, as if these individuals were speaking about me and to me alone, even though I was sitting with 50 others in the same room.

When I went to those meetings—sometimes despondent and confused about my life—I heard the exact messages I needed, as if God were talking directly to me, and for my benefit, through the innocent mouths of others. I believe those experiences saved my life. And because of this continued phenomenon, I've come to think that Spirit uses all of us as conduits for healing messages. Intuitively, I knew this to be the case, although if I tried to analyze it too much intellectually, I recognized that I was conflicted.

These situations are all examples of Cledons. It works today exactly as it did for the Romans, and for the Greeks before them, thousands of years ago.

Recently, I heard a very interesting story from a client's mother, Mary Rose, in Georgia, that illustrates this phenomenon beautifully. Mary Rose definitely got a Cledon in a grocery store. One day she was having a dinner party for her church group. She was planning to serve her signature chicken dish with peanut sauce, and she went to the grocery store to buy the ingredients for the recipe. Ted, the newly widowed minister, was receiving a lot of attention from the single women in the congregation, and Mary Rose was determined to bring her personal touch to the situation. Her peanut chicken would absolutely be the best meal this man had eaten in a while.

She sashayed down the aisle, excited that her mouthwatering sauce was going to outshine her friend Marvelle's barbequed pork dish, which had been such a hit the week before. Just as Mary Rose held the bag of peanuts in her hand, however, she noticed her hearing begin to amplify as two women walked slowly by her, having a discussion about food allergies.

She distinctly heard one woman say that her son Ted had almost died due to a severe allergic reaction to peanuts and how scary it was for the family. They had no idea he'd developed the allergy until he was ten years old. Mary Rose had a strong sensation that she should put the peanuts back, and an equally strong gut reaction that she'd heard the conversation as a warning. She quickly decided to make fried chicken instead.

That evening, Ted, the minister, praised her cooking and mentioned that his favorite food in the whole world was fried chicken just like she'd made for him. About then, one of the other ladies offered him a bowl of sugared mixed nuts she'd made. He declined and said, "Not unless you want a dead minister in the house. I haven't been able to eat those nuts since I was ten years old. I almost died in front of my mama, eating a candy bar."

Mary Rose almost fainted and excitedly told the story of Spirit sending her a spontaneous message through the two strangers at the grocery store. She'd received a Cledon! (It's a good thing she did—the minister proposed a couple of years later.)

This kind of message from Spirit only depends on intuitive receptivity and the willingness to listen. Mary Rose couldn't have known that Ted was allergic to peanuts. Even after she overheard the conversation, she still didn't know intellectually or rationally that he had an allergy. What *did* happen was that her senses were amplified in a noticeably different way. Even though she had no hard evidence that her chicken dish could have proven fatal, her intuitive knowing was strong. She'd learned to trust her hunches, so she listened. In the opinion and personal experience of Mary Rose, there was Divine purpose in that conversation. Although the women in the store were completely unaware of their part in the drama, they were used as oracles for the benefit of Mary Rose and, of course, the minister.

Spontaneous oracles delivered by innocent parties are the most common forms of Divine communication. They happen all the time to all of us, but even so, they depend on our capacity to receive with intuitive clarity, or at least on our paying attention. Unfortunately, it's just as common to ignore Cledons as coincidences or deny them as irrational and weird.

I heard a sad story about a California woman named Janet who'd been planning a trip to Lake Tahoe in her new RV. She was so excited about going and talked about it for weeks. She planned to pick up her boyfriend, Don, at his house early in the morning; and she took the preceding day off work so that she could pack.

The closer Janet got to finishing her packing, the more and more anxious she became. She had a strong sense that she shouldn't go on this trip and called her younger sister to tell her how she was feeling. As they talked, Janet heard music in the background and asked her sister what the song was. It was called "Please Don't Go."

Janet was startled and even laughed about it as a spooky coincidence, but then chose to ignore it. Nevertheless, she couldn't shake her sense of foreboding and went to sleep feeling uneasy and confused. In the morning as she washed her face, she still had the strong sense that she shouldn't go but decided that she was being silly and went to load the last of her bags.

She picked up Don as planned, and he said that he hadn't slept well but still wanted to drive. They turned on the radio, and a song came on called "Jesus, Take the Wheel." Trying to find a traffic report, they tuned in to another station . . . and the same song was playing: "Jesus, Take the Wheel." They both noticed the synchronicity of the event.

It was raining, so Don was driving carefully. As he turned a corner, a tractor-trailer skidded out of control, hit their RV, and knocked it over the railing into a ravine. Everyone involved ended up in the hospital with serious injuries. Janet's new camper was totaled, and Don permanently lost sight in one of his eyes.

Yet their caution paid off. You see, Don tended to be a reckless driver and more often than not exceeded the speed limit. He and Janet are convinced that hearing the messages in the songs made them more aware of their surroundings and saved their lives. Hindsight being 20/20, Janet recognized the Cledon in the first song that played while she was on the phone with her sister. "Please Don't Go" couldn't have been any more obvious—it was a wake-up call.

The Way a Cledon Works

Whether you ask one God or many aspects of that God, as they did in ancient Rome, Spirit will accordingly and truthfully answer whatever question you pose. Although Cledons can initially be engaged as interactive oracles, there's no way for any of us to know the form of the answer until we receive it. Cledons are seemingly sent spontaneously, and all you can do is be receptive to the manner in which Spirit chooses to send the message.

You can't ask a question, then go to the grocery store and pick two women having a conversation to be the messengers who will deliver the Cledon. Spirit may decide to answer you in a week while you're watching television or listening to the radio. You'll receive a message; but Spirit decides the how, when, and what.

My friend Kathy tells a hilarious story about how she ended up finding her very expensive diamond wedding ring, which she lost somewhere in her house. The night she realized it was missing, she called me in a panic, and I told her to pray for a sign and stay aware of any unusual amplification of her senses in the next little while. I told her that she might receive a message delivered through an innocent party whom she could hear over the radio, on television, or at the mall. She thought I was being ridiculous and got off the phone in a huff.

After tearing her house apart and not finding the ring, she begrudgingly prayed for a sign—and then she became depressed and truly annoyed with me when she didn't get any signs about her ring right away. She called a mutual friend to complain about me: "This praying stuff doesn't work! I don't know why I listen to those New Age 'woo woo' ideas. My wedding ring is a practical matter. Somebody stole it—I know that's what happened. Maybe the housekeeper did it."

Blah blah blah. So maybe the Cledon didn't come at her beck and call. What—it's my fault she prayed and nothing happened? I said to have patience, and decided I wasn't going to talk to her for a while.

Six weeks later, I got a sweet, happy phone call from my former nonbeliever friend. Turns out Kathy had tuned in to a made-for-television movie, and about ten minutes in, the female lead character dropped her wedding ring into the bathroom-sink drain. She called a plumber (who became her love interest) to fish it out.

What was uncanny to Kathy was that the garish wallpaper in the bathroom on the show was the exact pattern she'd removed from her powder room when she remodeled her house. That powder room was the one place she hadn't looked for her ring. Intuitively, she went there, peered into the sink's drain, and thought she saw something glitter. A plumber fished out her ring a couple of hours later. She didn't end up with the plumber (hubby was happy about that), but I got to say, "I told you so!" The common Cledon cleans up again!

I remember just a few weeks after meeting my husband, Marc, we were at a movie theater waiting for popcorn when I looked up at him and just had this strong sense that he was going to be my husband. He looked back at me and jokingly called me a "lovesick puppy"—like that was supposed to be cute. I was so mad at him for teasing me like that (even if it was true) that I marched to the bathroom to regroup. I told myself: *Forget it! I don't like to be teased like that.*

Then I heard a woman call to her friend in the next stall: "You are for sure going to marry that man. I just know it."

To which her friend replied, "I know I am, but it has to be his idea."

I will never forget that night. Of course I would marry Marc one day. Of course it had to be his idea. Thank God I'm a tenacious little Cancer crab girl. Patience when we want something is one of our astrological virtues, and I waited until it *was* his idea. He proposed on one knee, at night, in a gondola in Venice. I've come to love his ideas.

Spirit is always spontaneous when sending the common Cledon. Everybody gets them all the time, but most people don't even realize what they are. They're the only form of interactive oracle where you're meant to be completely passive. Tuning in to the Cledons in your life is fun and truly amazing once you get the hang of it.

So how do you recognize when it happens? When you receive a Cledon, it's as if Spirit knows exactly what's on your mind and then addresses it. Of course, Spirit knows everything that's going on with us because we're all part of Spirit. I'll repeat this over and over again, because it's the key to really understanding how the Divine conversation is possible.

Remember, Spirit is the primary component of us humans and of everything in the Universe. We're all here as individual manifestations of it. So in fact, Spirit is talking to itself when it sends us a message. Our souls—our higher selves, consciousness, or whatever else we call it—are plugged into the wisdom of Spirit. Our job is to tune in and listen because it's always talking to itself. There's a Divine dialogue going on all the time if we're willing to pay attention and participate.

Here's yet another example. Maggie was thinking of someone she hadn't seen for a while. Her old friend Loretta had been out of contact for a couple years, so it was odd that Maggie kept thinking of her for three days. On the third day, she was walking down the street and saw the name Loretta practically pop off a signpost and then heard someone behind her calling her name—"Maggie!" But it was another woman who answered. Then she heard another voice loudly saying, "Call me!"

Maggie sensed intensely that she must call Loretta. She did so later that evening and found that her friend had also been thinking of making contact. Loretta's mother had just passed in exactly the same way Maggie's had. Loretta felt only Maggie could have known what she was going through.

You might think these are just coincidences, but it was clear that the signs could have only meant something to Maggie. Her boyfriend, Bill, was with her at the time she got the messages, and none of them impacted him because they weren't directed at him. In fact, he didn't even remember the incident until Maggie insisted that her experience was guided by Spirit. He didn't notice the voice shouting "Call me!" at all, even though Maggie heard it as loud as could be. She saw, heard, and was compelled to act because the message intuitively felt personal and real. The name on the signpost was the most noticeable, vivid thing in sight, and the sound of the voice insisting "Call me!" floated high and distinct above the noise of the busy street. It was as if everything else went quiet so that she could listen through her *other knowing*. Yet again, a Cledon was delivered with a meaningful and transformative result.

The Common C'ledon

Moments of Synchronicity

When preparing to write this book, I prayed for a sign to show me who should be included, and Kathy Ryndak's name kept coming up. I'd met her many years ago and remember how at first sight I was struck by something about her. She glowed with a sparkly, golden, fuzzy light that I've come to recognize as a sign for me that Spirit is present. She has a calm goodness, as well as integrity and a real aura of compassion. I always enjoy chatting with her, however briefly, when we meet.

Kathy and her partner, Gord, are two of the most reputable and influential teachers in the New Age community in Toronto. Their school, the Transformational Arts College, attracts people from all over the world to study in-depth metaphysics, spiritual psychotherapy, music for healing, and alternative-healing methods. They've changed many lives in the 20 years they've been doing their work, and I have no doubt that they'll continue to do so.

Kathy's name kept coming up and up and up—so many times that I had to contact her to ask if she'd like to contribute. At least six people mentioned the name of her school over two days, and every coffee shop I went to had old copies of magazines with brilliant articles that she and her partner had written. These were billboards; not just signs.

In her own words, then, here is story from Kathy Ryndak.

> The first time I met Gord Riddell, my business partner at Transformational Arts College, I knew we would embark upon a profound spiritual journey that would come to transform my life and the lives of the thousands of students who would attend our school. A strong resonance of our energies and a deep inner knowingness signaled that we were meant to work and co-create together.
>
> Signs and symbols tend to come to me through people, events, my dog Chakra, and moments of synchronicity. When Gord and I were forming our spiritual partnership, I lived at the

119

corner of Marlee and Ridelle in Toronto. That was the Divine anonymously speaking to me and giving me the thumbs-up.

One summer day while resting under an oak tree, explaining the vision of the school and its name to a friend, the tree started to shower its acorns upon us. I laughed in amazement, never having witnessed this before, and I wondered what sign the universe was sending me. In Celtic mysticism, the oak represents inner fire, strength, spiritual nobility, and stepping through the "door" to create change.

The acorn is symbolic of huge potential in small things. That certainly is the story of the college. We started very small but have grown significantly over the years, embracing the art of alchemy and transformation through merging the fields of spirituality, psychotherapy, and holistic health.

I've always prayed for signs from the Universe, especially when decisions are hard to make or obstacles are in the way. "Show me a sign, Higher Self, show me the way," I'd say when asking for Divine guidance. When we first started the school, we promoted many speakers but weren't focused enough on developing our own material. While talking to Gord one day about why we weren't manifesting more, I posed the question, "Do you think we should be concentrating more on our own work?" Suddenly, a gust of wind blew the office window open, as if to answer my question. Indeed, many windows of opportunity did open for us when we shifted our focus to creating original material, since we were more aligned to our higher purpose.

I've learned that the Universe will always give us a sign when we put out the request. Often it's subtle, rather than the strike of a thunderbolt. Our challenge, then, is to listen to it and take insightful action.

CHAPTER 8

E.T.'S PHONE HOME?

One of my all-time favorite movies is Steven Spielberg's *E.T.: The Extra-Terrestrial,* about the little stranded alien who is befriended by a young boy. The phrase "E.T. phone home" from the movie reminded me of oracles. Like the extraterrestrial "phoning home," we earthbound terrestrials need to get in touch with our true origins, too. Home in our case is Spirit. Just as E.T. made a gadget to "phone home," so have we—lots of them. The impulse to "phone" and find "home" is what's really behind our request for direction in the Divine dialogue.

So many types of oracles, omens, and signs, yet so little time to talk about them all! One thing is for certain—the evolution of humanity has unfortunately made us numb to the extraordinary world of Spirit that we're all a part of. And we've lost much of the knowledge of how to dialogue with the Divine.

Looking back over thousands of years, we might imagine that we'd peer into a primitive and unsophisticated past, but that's an arrogant and foolish perspective. We may be advanced technologically; and we may live with greater comforts, gadgets, and all kinds of amenities, but in our progress we've lost sight of the truth that we are part of an ensouled world. It is Spirit first, then human (or animal, fish, plant, tree, or even rock).

There's a reason that the planet is referred to as Mother Earth! We seem to have forgotten that the planet is alive and that we're actually related to it as we are to every living thing. Even our human DNA is composed of the four elements of life found everywhere in our world: carbon, oxygen, hydrogen, and nitrogen.

We're all part of one living, Divine, intelligent energy that's individuated into various life-forms, like different members of the same family. All of us have a purpose, and although we appear separate, that's just an illusion that's leading us further from the truth. We need to remember what the ancients knew—that Spirit, the breath of God, is everywhere within us and around us, and is waiting to guide us. We just need to wake up.

We have a lot to learn from our ancient brothers' and sisters' beliefs and methods of spiritual dialogue. Since the beginning of recorded history, humans have always developed their faith and beliefs from what they observed. So going back thousands of years, we find evidence that ancient peoples believed that Spirit was living in Nature. The rich natural world was perceived to have immense unseen power and followed obvious patterns. Humankind found the sacred in the elements and saw the manifest power of Spirit everywhere.

They also experienced Spirit with "another knowing" that was accompanied by—but was separate from—their analytical minds. They were always aware of the power in the Unseen, and they had to rely on their intuition more than their intellect for survival. Because this constant intuitive exercise made people more receptive, they were also continually using oracular consciousness.

I believe that our ancestors had easy access to other dimensional realities that were lost as we evolved into an analytical, thinking, literate species, with our main focus being technological advancement. Ancient peoples found ways to express their active participation in Divine dialogue in the earliest forms of divination tools. They believed in the messages they sent and received because they saw and experienced evidence that they recognized.

Their observations of the sky are an interesting example of the development of a language for Divine dialogue. This was, of course, the birth of astrology in its earliest form. I had an intriguing conversation with my dear friend Robert Ohotto, intuitive astrologer and Hay House author. He said, "In looking to the celestial heavens to divine the will of the gods, we can actually trace the origins of modern-day astrology to the Babylonians."

The Babylonians occupied Mesopotamia from 2,000 B.C. to A.D. 0 in what is known today as Iraq. They believed that their gods communicated with them through the planets and stars via movements in the sky.

It's through these sky movements that they began interpreting the *omens,* or warnings, that the gods were giving them about what *might* happen—and what could be done to stay in harmony with universal design. The ancients believed that the gods were basically writing them letters in the sky to help them with their lives.

Divination began when people observed the symbolic communication from the world of Spirit. The saying "as above, so below" makes a whole lot of sense when we think about these Divine relationships. The myths and legends that fed the collective hunger for spiritual understanding were evolving stories that began when humankind first pondered the Mystery of God . . . and they continue growing today.

Divination was a way for us "terrestrials" to "phone home" and ask for guidance. We dialed up the gods and goddesses in the sky; we called our Goddess Mother out of the rocks and caves. We looked for Her in pools of water, in the blowing of the wind, and in the crackling of the fire.

We cast bones, threw stones with a sacred alphabet, and visited clairvoyant priestesses to get a message. We created sophisticated systems of symbology to connect to the ensouled world. We talked to animals and observed them for signs, and we asked a whole bunch of gods for advice until we finally just decided to divorce everybody else in the celestial family and only called on the big Daddy Heavenly Father. (Mom Goddess got left behind along the way.) Patriarchy and the silencing of the Divine feminine cast aside all reminders of the past. Then the action of dialing up Spirit became separated from its sacred nature; it was steeped in superstition and suspicion, and damned as heretical or evil.

The interesting thing is that no matter what we used or whom we thought we were talking to, somebody who loved us and wanted to dialogue with us picked up the Divine oracle phone. It might seem that with all our sophisticated progress, these old ways would have become obsolete and stopped working. Given the renewed strength of fundamentalism, we might believe that this subject would be rendered mute. Not so.

Spirit will answer today just as it would have back then. It remembers all our methods, and our basic questions have remained the same, although our challenges have changed along with us. The collective memory of all of humanity exists within Spirit like a big, invisible, living, conscious data bank. Forgetting isn't possible. Dial for the Divine and it will indeed pick up the phone. Remember, it answers by showing us mirror images of ourselves—we just need to know how to see the reflections. It's our soul that has the vision and the capacity for a deeper, more profound perception of reality.

Dial-Up Divine Mobile Services

Some ancient divination systems and oracular traditions still exist today. The most complicated ones are rich with symbolism and draw from ancient spiritual customs dating back thousands of years. I'd have to write an entire book on each one to do it justice. The point here is simply to introduce them and to acknowledge their continued presence in the current divinatory environment.

— **Astrology** is still alive and relevant now, although we're mostly exposed to a diluted form of the art in magazine horoscopes, which are more for entertainment than expressing its true purpose.

— **The Tarot** is an oracle system of divination created sometime in the 15th century. Nobody really agrees on its true origins, and many myths have been circulated about whether it may be thousands of years old rather than just hundreds. Bottom line: It's been around a while. This system uses 78 cards marked by complex symbols—some of which do date back thousands of years and are from a number of ancient sacred mystery traditions: Egyptian, Kabbalah, and others.

The Tarot is complicated, but if you're interested in the cards, I encourage you to just try them and see how your intuition leads you to the answers suggested by their symbolism. Books will give you the meanings, but I believe that using the cards is the only way you'll become familiar with their symbolic language and make them your own. (They can, however, hold a much deeper connection to the Divine if you commit to studying them in depth.) Because of their somewhat convoluted imagery, there can be a tendency to impose a mental influence on them—that is, it's easy to misinterpret them according to what you want to see instead of what's there. Nonetheless, they're helpful and can be extraordinarily accurate mirrors of your life and its direction.

With all divination systems, it's believed that you're being guided by Spirit as to what card, stone, or stick (or whatever object) you choose, and then the selected signs can be interpreted as the message. The Tarot, in even its most basic form, can also serve as an accurate means of reflecting your path. For example, I use the system to confirm story lines that I see clairvoyantly.

The cards serve as doorways into a deeper reflection of your journey and can provide missing details in the broader vista of intuitive sight. Entire books have been written about them; and if you're interested in learning more, authors Rachel Pollack and Mary Greer are two of many who have devoted much of their lives to the study and teaching of this rich and complex divination tool.

— **The *Book of Changes* (the *I Ching*)** is arguably the oldest, most venerated Chinese system of divination. Thousands of years old, it's still very much in circulation, with many modern transla-tions. Its interpretive insights depend on the toss of coins or sticks that are compared to 64 hexagrams and interpreted according to their changing development from one divinatory meaning that evolves into another. Again, it's impossible to do more than men-tion it here. I've studied the *I Ching* for years and still don't know it in its entirety. If it intrigues you, then be prepared to spend a while getting to know the system. It will surprise you.

— **Ancient Norse runes** were made popular again 20-some years ago by author Ralph Blum. This oracle system uses stones with a symbolic alphabet that, when tossed, will give very accu-rate information about your life.

I love my Runes and use them when I really want to be clear about a situation. I don't always like what they say, but they've never once been wrong in reflecting where I am and where I'm heading. In fact, what I really like best about them is that my mind can't mix up the meanings to end up the way I want.

If you're interested in knowing more about this divination sys-tem, there are lots of books and resources available thanks to the Internet. One of the best metaphysical resources online is **www. crystalinks.com**. This site is a wonderful place to do some more in-depth study about all things relating to oracles, omens, signs, and any other similar subjects.

— **Sacred numerology** is making a comeback, which I'll talk about in more detail later.

— **Kabbalah**, the ancient Jewish mystery school with its own divinatory and oracular traditions, has attained modern celebrity status with Madonna as its poster girl.

— Visiting the oracle at Delphi, a venerated tradition that lasted some 1,400 years in ancient Greek civilization, has mor-phed in our current culture in the form of **psychics, mediums,** and **intuitives.** These modern oracle messengers have their own hit radio and television shows and speak at sold-out seminars and on luxury cruises for spiritual growth and development. I happen to be so fortunate as to be included among those.

— **Animal communicators** provide phone consults for your ailing or troubled pet.

Whether you greet all this with faith or skepticism, oracles and the interpreting of omens and signs are alive and well today.

Divination Dial-Up in the Past

For fun, I thought you might like to know a couple of additional ways in which humankind has made contact with the Divine. Some examples of divinatory practices are often greeted by sounds like *eeuww* or *yuck,* and others by heads nodding in reverent remembrance or excited possibility. I'm sure you'll have no trouble figuring out which is which.

The practice of reading entrails from a sacrificed animal died out quickly, thank goodness. However, reading signs in animal livers continued to be a very common practice in Greece, Rome, Babylon, and other ancient cultures. (Both practices have a very big *yuck* factor.) The reading of livers continued to be a clandestine method up until the mid-1500s (although it could have gone on longer) in Catholic countries such as Spain, Italy, and France. Note the word *clandestine*—very few people came out of the "liver divining" closet in those days, although there are numerous historic accounts that attest to its presence.

No wonder divination was given a bad name. Who would think someone was speaking to God while staring into a dead cow's liver, looking for signs of spiritual guidance. *Here's a liver. Now let's see if Spirit is sending us a message?* I imagine that the liver might have said, "Avoid the inquisitor and think of another way to dial up. Your program is obsolete!"

We do know that the intention and sacred quality of the practice became corrupted, and eventually this divinatory system died out altogether, as it was meant to. Maybe that's what the Bible means by fortune-telling: It's what happens when the sacred and the Divine are removed from the dialogue. Regardless, it's not something that has relevance today, for which I'm personally relieved.

Why Divination, Oracles, Omens, and Signs Are Still Going Strong

The modern fascination with the spiritual, the supernatural, and other worlds can be witnessed in our most common art forms—television and film—spanning the past 40 years or so. They show that we're thinking about all of this since that's the way we choose to entertain ourselves. *Bewitched, I Dream of Jeannie, The Ghost & Mrs. Muir, Medium, Ghost Whisperer, Charmed, Angel, Touched by an Angel,* and *Supernatural* are only some of the most popular ways that we've stayed connected to the potential "otherness" in life and to Spirit.

The wild success of books such as *The Da Vinci Code* and the Harry Potter series speak loudly to the modern world's need for new stories and myths as we question our old ones. C. S. Lewis and J. R. R. Tolkien made us all believers in Narnia and Middle-earth and kept the wonder of the beauty of Christian myths—and of the continuing battles between the Light and dark—alive in our hearts. Books like *The Mists of Avalon* by Marion Zimmer Bradley remind us to look to the past for the forgotten spiritual treasure of the Divine feminine. Remember, there's a Goddess to the God, or at least there once was. Time to bring her back, I'd say.

We need to know that there's magic in the world. We need to know—not just hope—that good will one day overcome evil. We all want to have our own "prophecy jars" like the glass bubble that contained a prophecy for Harry Potter; we long for something to speak to us like that. We'd love to know that unicorns still roam the forest. How wonderful to be chosen by an animal companion like the way Hedwig the owl chose Harry. And we all want the soul contracts drawn between the daemons (or visible portions of the human spirit, appearing as animals) and their human counterparts in *The Golden Compass* by Philip Pullman.

Even in the romance-novel genre, there has been an increase in bestsellers with paranormal story lines. In them, not only can the heroine pray for an angel to guide her, but she can fall in love with him when he shows up. And yes, angels even give up their wings to marry these women—after they've gotten rid of the bad guys. In many of these popular new novels, the characters have knowledge of ancient sacred traditions of divining, which they use to help them in their adventures—and in greater service to all of humankind.

We need these stories to reflect symbolically where we are in the forever-evolving relationship between our mortal selves and the place where our immortal souls reside. Inherently, we have a sense that we belong to a greater living Spirit, which connects us to the earth and all other living things, even if our world keeps us focused on fear and separation. Deep within us, we know that we're sleeping and that the frozen ground of winter is waiting for the thaw of spring. Then we can wake up and be lucid and present to the beauty of the soul's experience.

So however we create an environment to maintain contact with Spirit and the ensouled world—whether it's through fanciful fiction or deep philosophical inquiry—it's a sign that we want to remember what we forgot. It's a sign that something important is stirring within us, even if we're unsure of where to begin to look for our missing link. It indicates that we're longing to be awake to our Divine nature and in a sacred conversation with Spirit.

What can help us connect to our inner oracular consciousness and find our answers and good guidance? How can we recognize when Spirit aligns events, people, and experiences in Divine synchronicity? What in the natural world still speaks to us and invites us to see with clearer and more vivid vision? Even if we don't receive some deep, great mystical revelation, perhaps it can just tell us that deciding against a trip was a good idea or that it's in our family's highest good to send our child to another school. It's in the minute details of mundane life that we play out our greater archetypal personal destinies. Consider that those seemingly tiny, insignificant moments are the things that Spirit cares about.

How to Prepare to Use Interactive Oracles in Divining the Will of Spirit

The quality of your dialogue with Spirit begins with the quality of your intention. Ask for Divine guidance in a reverent and respectful manner. When you decide to use an interactive oracle or divination tool, be prepared with the understanding that you're approaching the Sacred and not a "supernatural slot machine" rigged to tell you everything you demand to know. You're meant to be asking for a higher view of things; and in doing so, you're sure to find your connection to these sacred places within you. You must be aware and accept when you enter the dialogue that it may lead not to answers, but to even deeper questions. Part of your soul's contract may be to discover the solutions for yourself.

We're not going to ask, "Hey, Spirit, what's it gonna be? When am I gonna win the lottery?" That said, I'm sure many people have visited oracles, asked for a sign, or prayed to God to grant their wishes and gotten answers. But there's a caution here: We pay a price for asking without a higher purpose. It's easy to get caught in the desire to know the future in order to get an edge on life or to prevail over others, but it may not be in our highest good to have that knowledge.

There are times, though, when Spirit reveals the future so that we can take action to prevent a tragedy or to shed illumination on an important decision, impacting many. When future events are revealed it's because we're meant to see them, and those times we're truly blessed. (Yet we can only really know *how* blessed once we get there.)

Spirit messages can come in strange ways. I remember a particular visit to Los Angeles when all week long I ran into people who claimed that my perspective of their futures had, in fact, turned out to be very detailed and accurate. Someone asked me how I could see those things, some of which had been dismissed as being impossible when I spoke of them years before. I was pondering the question, since I only have my theories. It remained on my mind and became the constant background noise to my thoughts. *How is the future seen?* I must have asked myself the question 100 times a day that week. It was actually starting to irritate me because I couldn't seem to turn it off.

This is how Spirit answered me. I was staying at Le Montrose Suite Hotel in West Hollywood, my favorite L.A. lodgings. I had two strange incidents with the television in my room as Spirit was having fun rearranging the programming for my benefit. In the first case, I turned on the TV to watch a show about crop circles while I was waiting for my girlfriend Cecil to visit. I was fascinated by the show and watched it until 5:45 P.M., when the doorbell rang.

I greeted Cecil and told her excitedly about the crop-circles documentary. I said that we should order dinner and watch it together. We entered the room and lo and behold, the screen was showing *Jeopardy!* I thought I might have accidentally switched the channel, so we went through them all, but there was nothing like what I'd seen earlier. Over dinner, we wondered what had happened to the show, assuming it was my hotel programming that screwed it up.

In fact, the program wasn't supposed to be shown until two hours later, which I discovered when I turned the television back on and had a *déjà vu* experience. Cecil went home and checked the *TV Guide,* then called to tell me I couldn't possibly have seen the show while I was waiting for her because it wasn't on any station until 8:30 P.M.—much later than when she'd arrived. And so I listened to her wonderful laugh, and she called me a "weirdo," but in an affectionate way.

And the message was? No, the hotel doesn't have a special theme room for *The Twilight Zone* that I get when I stay there. Nothing that I could personally decipher about this incident made any sense, other than maybe Spirit was having some fun with me.

Even stranger was the experience I had during the same trip when I went to sleep watching *The Sopranos* . . . or so I thought. At that point I wasn't a fan of the show and only watched it occasionally, so I wasn't familiar with the current plot.

I returned to Canada, and then a month or so later, my husband and I had dinner with our friend Gerry and his wife, Pam, who were both avid fans of the mob drama. Talking about it, I mentioned I'd seen an episode where Carmela was in the kitchen talking to Tony about a bear in the backyard. I remembered that the couple was separated. Pam looked at me and said, "That's not the story line."

Maybe the U.S. gets *The Sopranos* before Canada does? We discussed what a shame it was that we didn't get HBO at the same time as our neighbors to the south. And then we forgot all about it until the following year when the new season of *The Sopranos* began—with the show that I couldn't possibly have seen when I did, because it didn't exist at that point. All four of us were witnesses to the conversation where I let the cat out of the bag—without having a clue that I'd done so. Of course, I became a fan of the show on the spot!

Was Spirit soliciting me to become a *Sopranos* fan? I don't think so. I think the time-space experience sometimes just gets a little weird for those of us who spend many of our waking hours exploring the other realms of Spirit. I have no clue why I got a sneak preview of a show I didn't even watch at the time. Yet it did answer my curiosity about how the future could be seen. I seem to have gotten a pretty bizarre but direct answer—the future is seen on TV. Very funny. (Spirit has a warped sense of humor.)

The point of these anecdotes is to remind us all about discernment. Some messages are deeply meaningful, some just are what they are and don't mean more than that, and some—well, some are just great little nudges. They tell us that there's definitely more to the unseen realm than there is to the world we see. After all, I asked, "How is the future really seen?" and Spirit showed it on a hotel-room television. Okay, I get it.

Australian Aborigines believe that dreamtime is our real life and this "reality" is actually the illusion. We might learn a little something from their viewpoint that many worlds stand beside each other, sometimes overlapping. And that can translate into *The Sopranos* and the crop-circles documentary that really existed in another place, giving me a nudge back in *my* place. I think.

Prayer

Prayer is essential when exploring the world of oracles, omens, and signs because it sets up the conversation. It's how you make a statement to Spirit (God, Goddess, *I Am* Presence, Christ Consciousness) that you humbly commit to the Light when asking for guidance. The prayer should be first a statement of intention, then a request to be protected from harm, and finally a petition for the will of the Divine to be revealed. If there's a specific situation that you're inquiring about, name it to see if Spirit will show you a reflection of what you can't see on your own. Remember to approach contact with oracular wisdom with humility, not demands. Spirit decides the manner in which it answers you, and it will reflect where you are at every given moment.

Before people use the card deck and divination system that I created, which is called *The Wisdom of Avalon Oracle Cards*, I encourage them to bless their cards with an invocation to the Goddess, which I wrote specifically for that purpose:

> *Dear Goddess, I invoke your power of love and discernment*
> *as I use these cards to guide me along the path to Avalon*
> *and my soul, and for the manifestation of my true purpose for*
> *the greatest good. Show me only what is best and true for*
> *myself and for others. Let only light shine. Blessed be.*

A general prayer requesting guidance from Spirit, using any oracle system, can be something along these lines:

*Spirit, I'm here humbly asking to see the truth of my reflection
in your message for the highest good of all. Let there be Light,
and show me the way of my true path, if it be thy will.*

Or you can pray:

*I invoke the blessings, protection, and guidance of the
eternal <u>I Am</u> Presence. Let there be Light. If it be thy will, please
show me what I need to know about my situation to stay
true to my path for the highest good of all.*

Or perhaps you might say:

*I offer myself to the highest good. Show me what you will.
Show me what I need to know today [about such and such].*

You can also create a prayer of your own with words that mean
something sacred to you, always asking for the highest good and
for the will of Spirit to guide you.

Sometimes Spirit sends a message just to let you know it's present and aware of you. Those moments are doorways in your soul
that you're invited to consciously enter in order to be reminded of
the importance of your spiritual life. When led by prayer and by
requesting the connection in this way, the door to the soul's receptive knowing is open and the ensouled world becomes ready to be
explored.

Meditation

Meditation is something I encourage as a means to slow down
and contemplate the Divine. Also, there are many forms that are
effective in helping clear blocks to the intuitive reception necessary to receive, accept, and decipher messages from Spirit. My
CD *Journey Through the Chakras* was created specifically with this
intention. All the guided-visualization exercises that accompany

my first book, *Remembering the Future,* may be downloaded for free from my Website, **www.colettebaronreid.com**. Guided meditations are especially good if you have trouble concentrating. No matter what form of meditation you practice—Zen, TM, mindfulness meditation, or guided—I encourage you to develop a daily ritual as an essential component of engaging Divine dialogue.

Also, always meditate on any answer you receive. Stilling your mind's chatter and quieting your desire to interpret something to fit a certain way will reveal the true nature of an oracle message, sign, omen, or circumstance. Contemplation of the sign will show you its deeper meaning in the context of your life.

Now let's get into how to start the conversation with Spirit. I'm very sure that Spirit has lots to tell you.

PART III

The Divine
Toolbox of
Interactive
Oracles

CHAPTER 9

DIVINING THE MAP
OF YOUR LIFE

Since we come to Spirit asking for guidance and knowledge about the path we're on, wanting to know the outcome of some of our choices, we need to keep in mind a few important points: Each life has a set of lessons and themes that play out as a backdrop to our journey. We're here to learn, and we're all different.

Imagine that before you were born you chose a contract with your soul to experience certain aspects of being human for one lifetime. You forgot about the soul as soon as you incarnated. You've spent your life learning to remember who you really are—spirit first, human second. When you're born, you're handed a multidimensional map with layers of terrain that intersect at different places. When you look at your map, imagine that you'll see an X and a sign saying "You Are Here."

So now suppose that some of your journey was preplanned before you got here, and it's marked in red along a particular set of roads. This map of the route you're supposed to travel shows the physical terrain and various other aspects of the land. You notice mountains, rivers, and marshes; or maybe your road goes alongside the ocean or into caves. The bottom line is that you see the path you're meant to follow, with all the possible side trips or detours. The unpredictable part is which way you choose to go.

You see intersections where you're supposed to meet particular individuals or have certain experiences that are key to your soul's contract. Your fate will come to pass in those events that are meant to be. I believe that certain things will happen according to fate, and certain life themes will play out as well. A detailed astrology chart will show you the themes of your contract as you evolve on your journey.

There's no "real" map, of course, only speculative trends and influences that can be known in advance to aid in your personal growth. Certain life experiences are contracted to happen, and they *will* occur—no matter how you may try to avoid them. Those fated experiences are crucial; it's as if they were encoded with special "wake-up bells."

Your destiny appears as you respond and react to the challenges and opportunities that fate brings. It's as if Spirit has preprogrammed a whole bunch of messages that you're meant to receive on your life path. These are also moments where a window of opportunity opens so that you can choose to make a change to another path. They don't last long, but they are indeed offered.

Using Your Map

Divination can act as a means to track those points of intersection so that you can actively create the conditions for a more beneficial life. Spirit will always show you clues and signs as you track your journey. You just need to know how to read their markers.

There's another way to look at this sacred map. Consider the possibility of other realities and dimensions overlapping and running parallel to this one. From what I understand, in the contemporary scientific community there's an "accepted emerging consensus" of the existence of "multi-verses": parallel, correlating dimensions of reality that exist simultaneously with this one. No longer do we see the universe as a single expanse; rather, it's understood to be more complex and vast than previously known.

In his book *The Isaiah Effect,* Gregg Braden (who's decidedly one of my most important influences) mentions the work of Hugh Everett III, the pioneering physicist from Princeton University, who was the first to name this phenomenon and way ahead of his time. "Everett went so far as to give a name to the moments in time where the course of an event can be changed. He called these windows of opportunity 'choice points,'" says Braden. "The choice point is like a bridge making it possible to begin one path and change course to experience the outcome of a new path."

So can we influence these choice points, or do they just show up as fated and preordained? In fact, through our inherent spiritual power—with our intentions, thoughts, beliefs, and emotions—we can create conditions to attract these choice points. We then can experience ourselves in a different reality by having some conscious part in creating it.

What science has found echoes what I'm illustrating with the map concept. Along with the most obvious road to travel are others that can be found through the magical doorways of awareness. These come with the alignment of conditions created by our thoughts, feelings, and emotions. There are many points along the way that open up so that we can choose new roads and opportunities. When we ask Spirit for illumination, oracles and the symbolic language of omens and signs also can serve as catalysts to let us know how to participate in the process and initiate change to a higher, life-affirming experience.

We don't create and experience life in a vacuum. I can think of so many people who have been fated to show up in my life. I always have the exact same feeling about them, too—it's as if the moment I set eyes on them becomes frozen in time and I can take a photograph of it. The space-time continuum seems to have a temporary slowdown, and all my senses become keenly aware that this person is—or will be—important to my life in some way.

Divine Intersections and Fate: Keep a Journal

Keep a journal of those moments when fate seemed to step into your life and the points when radical change was possible. This a great way to learn to pay attention to when such times happen again in the future. The details of your contract become apparent as you learn the lessons triggered by fate. You begin to understand those choice points taken or not taken, and how the experiences have influenced your journey to date.

I've been journaling for 40 years pretty consistently, and I can trace the moments of fate as my life intersected with others' lives. I also know the exact points when I was given an instant in time to change course, take a leap, or opt to walk another path. Great, important lessons that have helped strip me of my illusions can easily be seen there. My own personal soul's contract became clear over time as I observed my experience.

Your own *fate and Divine intersections journal* will really help you focus on how Spirit sends you people or events to help you learn. You can also get a clear picture of when time stood still and another reality was there for the choosing. Some things won't be so pleasant; others will have appeared as gifts.

Use your journal to examine these questions and statements:

1. Starting at childhood, can you recall which people seemed fated to enter your life?

2. Describe the feeling of first meeting them.

3. How did each person help you become aware of your true nature?

4. Describe the lessons learned from each person coming into your life.

5. What message do you believe was being sent to you by Spirit to help you grow?

6. From childhood to the present, describe the patterns you see triggered by fate.

7. Repeat the same exercise, only describing fate through specific events.

8. How does Spirit most often choose to get your attention?

9. How does fate influence your path today?

10. Make a list of all the times in your life when you know that you experienced a choice point.

11. What did you do? What choice did you make? How did your life change or not change by becoming aware of the opportunity to completely alter your course?

This exercise will help you understand the kinds of questions and guidance most needed on your journey. The more you understand about your path, the deeper your relationship to Spirit. You'll come to know the right questions to ask when participating in the conversation.

You can always expect some kind of response in a dialogue with the Divine. Why not talk about something important? Instead of asking, *Is he going to be my boyfriend?* you'll know to ask, *What are the lessons I need to learn through this potential relationship?* You may get an answer that in fact, you don't need the potential lessons because you've learned them already. You may get the response that the lesson is about harmonious partnership and love, and how to balance power between two people. This approach also avoids Yes/No answers and helps you as you move on to the other interactive oracles in the coming chapters.

CHAPTER 10

WAITER, THERE'S A MESSAGE IN MY SOUP

The art of reading images and symbols in leftover coffee grounds, as my father used to do, is an ancient Middle Eastern tradition closely related to tea-leaf reading, which actually had its beginnings in China. In fact, there's evidence that this kind of coffee or tea divination evolved independently in ancient cultures all over the world, including those of Asia, Greece, and the Middle East. It seems that everybody saw things in their cups! The official name for this practice is tasseography, or tasseomancy.

Over the last few hundred years, it became known throughout Europe because of the nomadic people who offered it as a means of telling fortunes. Okay, so now we find something related to the interpretations of Divine dialogue being "fortune-telling," but the beginnings of this art were sacred and accompanied by ritual prayer and meditation. Its purpose was to seek deeper knowledge of the will of the Divine and to glimpse where we were on our life's journey.

Tasseography can be a very accurate means of seeing the patterns and choices playing out in your life. It's like a map of encoded sacred symbols unfolding around the cup or saucer. It tells stories and depends upon your intuition for unlocking their code.

This is one reason that cups are traditionally read by someone other than the person drinking the tea or coffee. It's always better to have an objective perspective, and it serves to engage the connecting bridge between the consciousness of the person getting the reading and the person acting as interpreter. It's in this partnership that oracular consciousness is ignited and linked to the greater consciousness of Spirit.

Here's a story from a friend about a coffee-grounds reading that sounded an alarm.

> A few years ago, I went to visit my aging mother in Europe. For the first time, I was forced to leave my teenage son and daughter alone in the house for three whole weeks, and I was very worried about it. As a precaution, I asked my friend Nina to look after my children and help them if they needed anything.
>
> I arrived at my mother's house on a Saturday afternoon, and a friend of hers, Julie, visited us. As is the custom there, we each had a cup of Turkish coffee. After we finished, Julie offered to read our coffee grounds. She looked in my cup and showed me the silhouette of a pretty little house with a female figure standing to the left of it, and a male figure standing to the right. Both were looking at it. Julie commented that they were probably my son and daughter, and according to her, everything looked quiet and peaceful. That calmed me down a little.
>
> Two days later, on Monday, Julie returned and repeated the reading. This time there was just the lower part of the pretty house in the coffee grounds—the roof was gone. The figures were still there, but pale and barely visible. She said that although the roof wasn't apparent, she felt that everything was still okay and that both figures were safe.
>
> I felt uneasy, so I tried calling home, but nobody answered. Then I called Nina, and I couldn't reach her either. More than 24 hours went by as I kept calling. I began to panic and contacted everybody I knew back home. Finally, a friend informed me that Nina's house had been destroyed by a fire just a few

hours after Julie first saw the shapes in my coffee cup. Nina and
her husband lost their home, but as Julie predicted, they weren't
physically harmed by this ordeal. My children, thankfully, were
absolutely fine.

As my dad used to say, the soul and the mind need to get together in order to know the whole picture. So intuition (the voice of the inner teacher/guardian that is your soul), coupled with the capacity for symbolic thought and analysis and applied to the physical substance in the cups, equals the miracle of divination. You can receive valid, profound, accurate, and meaningful information, as well as have fun! This is a very social form of asking Spirit for guidance since you always need two or more people. It's also a way to experience Spirit "instant messaging" you through yet another natural substance—this time the tea leaves or the fine coffee grounds.

Once you know the symbols and their meanings (see the guide in Chapter 17), you'll be amazed by how easy and accurate the stories are that want to speak through the cups!

Beyond Teacups and Coffee Mugs

You can use the same method to chat with Spirit via thick hot chocolate or any kind of pureed vegetable soup. You can even use the leftover hot oatmeal in your breakfast bowl, as long as you pray for guidance and ask Spirit to be engaged.

Here's a funny story about the birth of the soup oracle. I actually stumbled upon the capacity for thick squash soup to be a conduit for a message from Spirit eight years ago. My eyesight began to get weak around the time I turned 42. Although I needed glasses, I avoided getting them—which, of course, gave me splitting headaches and made me squint when looking at small print. Seeing into a cup accurately was difficult without glasses since the symbols and images formed by the tea leaves and coffee grounds are tiny.

I promised a girlfriend who was visiting from Europe that I'd read her Turkish-coffee cup as a gift for her birthday. We thought it would be fun to go out for dinner first, and then at the end of the evening we'd return to my place to speak to Spirit via the cup. It was fall, and we went to a restaurant that was serving seasonal vegetable dishes. We both ordered squash soup, which arrived in large white bowls. As we were eating, I noticed the obvious patterns that were forming, and I began to peer along the sides of my bowl. I saw a clear image of a swan, followed by a pumpkin, then a baby.

Symbolically, the swan represents transformation and also clairvoyance, the ability to use intuitive vision to see beyond the here-and-now, as well as deep within to unseen places. It is my main personal animal totem. The pumpkin jumped out at me like a hologram and was clearly letting me know that Spirit wanted to speak through the medium of the squash. I interpreted the baby as something born new. So I told her that we'd do her reading using the soup!

I said a prayer and asked that I be given vision to see and receive whatever Spirit wanted to reveal for my friend. I asked her to turn her bowl three times clockwise on the dinner plate it was resting on, then turn it upside down toward herself. (The waiter wasn't impressed, but my friend was about to be.) I asked her to pass me the overturned bowl and plate and, after letting it sit for two or three minutes, I turned it over and proceeded to read the images in the bowl and on the plate. This was exactly the method I was taught for reading tea leaves or coffee grounds.

The best part about all of this was that the images were nice and large, very readable, and I didn't have to squint to figure out the symbols. It was as if Spirit was letting me know that I found a squash-soup version of those large-print paperback books. Forget the coffee or tea—get some soup! Never mind the reading glasses, either (although now that I'm pushing 50, I have to wear them for sure).

Needless to say, the soup oracle was right on and yet again an example to remind me that Spirit is everywhere we ask it to be.

All of the signs and omens I read were accurate in describing what was going on in my friend's life, and we were both excited that the new soup oracle actually worked! However, she vehemently rejected one interpretation. I got an image of a stork and a cradle, which obviously led me to ask if she was trying to have a baby. She replied that she was *absolutely not.* In fact, she'd just met someone and they'd only begun their physical relationship. I did know that because I also saw the relationship unfolding with potential.

So other than the scary comment about pregnancy, all was well, and off we went home. The next day I got a phone call from my friend, who was in hysterics. She hadn't been able to shake my mentioning the stork and baby images, so she stopped and bought three different pregnancy tests before going back to her hotel, just to calm her nerves. In the morning, she took all three tests. Oh well, soup doesn't lie—there was indeed a baby!

So how does Spirit respond to our queries through bowls of soup, coffee grounds, or tea leaves? It answers because it's been there all along. Spirit is within all things, and all of Life can be used as sacred mirrors for us to gaze into and see ourselves from another perspective in the unfoldment of our journeys. The Greater Consciousness can be engaged and known anywhere, anytime.

Another great example of this happened with a woman who attended one of my seminars on a cruise. During the lunch break, I told everybody to get in groups of four to six people and ask their bowls of pea soup to show something valid about their lives. We began this process by offering a prayer, spending a few moments contemplating the Divine, then asking for guidance and the ability to see the pea soup as ensouled with Spirit.

One woman came to me with her bowl and I immediately saw a bonsai tree, which seemed to be important. She was, indeed, obsessed with the plants and was hoping to get some for her home. It was a sign from Spirit that she'd made contact—however mundane—with the sacred mirror.

Meanwhile, at another table, an astounding thing was happening. A lovely woman named Nancy had been recently widowed. She'd come on the cruise to ease her pain and to connect with other spiritual seekers of like mind. Imagine her surprise when it was her turn, and she passed her bowl around to the other five women who were all strangers and who knew nothing about her. Each one in turn saw the same things, exclaiming:

"Look at the happy faces! And I see a man with a long, bushy beard."

"Me, too, and it seems that he's very tall as well."

"Yes, I see happy faces there, there, and there. Yes, a man's face smiling with a long, bushy beard."

Nancy was in shock and overwhelmed by the miracle of the message she knew was real. Her husband collected "happy faces" and was a very distinct individual—tall and burly with a very long and bushy beard.

My friend Mary Aver in London sent me another wonderful story about how other foods can become oracles when the traditional tea leaves or coffee grounds are nowhere to be found. Mary is an Irish shaman and a very accurate and effective clairvoyant counselor who leads seminars, writes, and does pretty much what I do. This story is about peanuts.

Tea-leaf reading was a common practice in my family home, and it was usual for Auntie Nora to read our cups when the family gathered around the kitchen table at supper. These were the days when tea was made with "proper tea," as my mother called it, as opposed to tea bags. Some took Auntie Nora with a pinch of salt, while I regarded her as the wisest woman I knew. She'd say to me, "You know your way around this world." I discovered that I knew something of this ancient practice, too, and I listened and watched Auntie Nora with great focus. I learned how to read teacups and coffee cups; it was great fun and enlightening, too.

I found out that this was an authentic way of accessing information that was hidden in our psyches. It was a tool for tapping into the subconscious and discovering what lies there.

One day not so long ago on a train from Cairo bound for Aswân in lower Egypt, an Egyptian gentleman requested that

I read for him. He was our tour guide, and when I looked into his eyes, I recognized that he needed to learn something. But I didn't have leaves of any kind available.

He had in front of him a bag of peanuts. Pointing to them, I asked him to hold them in his hands and think about the question that was foremost in his mind. Then he "cast" them on the table and waited. I discovered that day that I could read these cast peanuts as though they were leaves or coffee grains! The information was in fact useful and assisted this man in understanding a legal issue that involved his family. And it was then I recognized that perhaps it wasn't the leaves that were important. It may be possible to read any item connected to the person having a reading.

I did wonder what Auntie Nora thought of it all as she looked on from beyond the sky.

On Your Own

So how can you receive messages from Spirit in the same way? Here's what you need to do:

1. Find a partner to translate and interpret the images. Or even better, a group of four to six friends can meet once a week for a month to spend some time getting to know the Guide to the Sacred Sign-Bearers in Chapter 17.

2. Get a white soup bowl and put it on top of a dinner plate.

3. Use pea or squash soup, or any other soup that's pureed and thick. This can also be done with very thick hot chocolate in a white mug. It even works with mashed potatoes and thick gravy!

4. Begin with a prayer. Yes, I'm suggesting a very heathen thing to do—praying to the Spirit within the soup (and no laughing allowed). Thank the earth for the vegetables in the soup that will give you

nourishment. Then envision the life force of the veggies; see that energy as part of Gaia, part of the world, part of the universe, and made of Spirit. Bless the soup as a sacred instrument of life, and ask Spirit to reveal whatever message or image it has for you.

5. After you eat your soup, turn the bowl clockwise three times then gently turn the bowl upside down and toward you. Some of the contents will spill onto the plate, but a lot will stick to the sides of the bowl and form patterns. Let the bowl sit upside down for about three minutes, or until the residue has dried.

6. Remember that this exercise is first and foremost a way for you to reconnect to Spirit in all things. You engage your own oracular consciousness as you allow your awareness to expand and accept the vast connectivity among all things seen and unseen.

7. Now the fun part: Taking turns, pass one person's bowl around the group; if there are two of you, switch with your partner. You'll see patterns in the residue along the inner sides of the bowl and on the dinner plate. What do you see? Allow your inner mind to open and unfold. You'll know when this happens as your intuition ignites and oracular consciousness begins to recognize the symbols. Tell a story as you see it unfold. Then discuss it with your friends and see how it fits in their lives.

When there are more people the story can become more active as all participants engage their higher senses to see what's mirrored in the soup. Sometimes very mundane things are shown (like the person wants a bonsai tree), but other times deep and profound insights can be experienced when Spirit sends messages via the sacred mirror of a blessed bowl of soup.

CHAPTER 11

FINDING YOUR ANIMAL TOTEMS

When our ancestors lived closer to the earth and knew the relationships between all living things, they recognized that each animal, insect, reptile, tree, plant, and flower had certain properties that gave them power, and that every living thing was part of the integral balance of all of Life. Every one of these was seen and understood to have a potent spirit. That hasn't changed; it's just that over time our perception of it has. We've accepted the physical and the spiritual as separate and unrelated. This isn't the truth at all.

As Ted Andrews—the storyteller and mystic who works with birds of prey—says, "We cannot separate the physical from the spiritual, the visible from the invisible."

Although we live in a highly advanced technological and scientific culture, Spirit is still inherent and immanent within all of Life, whether we choose to include it in the current version of our worldview or not. Our just saying that things are a certain way doesn't mean that's the way it is. We can't see the oxygen in the air, but it's still there. It isn't visible, but we all know that without it we'll die. Where are our thoughts? If we can't see where they're stored or how they're generated, do they not exist? Consciousness is everywhere. Science has proven that we're made of the same substance as the stars. Are we then not stars looking at the stars?

If we observe the world around us quietly, patiently, and with reverence, we'll see how Consciousness (or Spirit) speaks to us through all forms of life using the archetypal energies within each of them as a language.

Many times throughout my life, ever since I was very young, a swan has come to visit me both when I've been sleeping and when I've been awake and daydreaming. I've also been deeply connected to the wolf. I've dreamed of these animals leading me out of difficulties. Also, sometimes a dolphin swimming beside me has helped me breathe when I've woken up gasping for air.

Until I studied shamanism and Native American spiritual traditions, I had no idea of the significance of the animals that came to me. I've since learned that the swan is known as a sign of transformation, developing intuition, and being able to see the future. It also symbolizes poetry, mysticism, and song. I see now that this totem—the name for any natural object, animal, or life-form you have an affinity with—was, and is, a powerful sign for me. The archetypal symbolism of the swan has followed me since I was born and has inspired everything that I do, especially now.

Clairvoyant natural healer Christine Agro had an up-close-and-personal encounter with an animal totem.

The Messenger

I was living in a beautiful log cabin in the Adirondacks, and I took a break to sit and meditate. As I sat silently, off and on I kept hearing a "thwapping" sound. Finally I got up to investigate, and the sound led me to the mudroom. There, sitting on the potting ledge, was a red-tailed hawk. As I entered, he flew to the window and beat his wings against it in an attempt to get out. I spoke quietly to him and told him that I'd help; I asked him to trust me. I reached my hands out slowly and gently wrapped them around his body, holding his wings.

For a moment, time stopped as I held this beautiful creature in my hands and looked deep into his eyes. As I got to the door of the room (which was open, fortunately), I released my hands. He didn't fly off immediately. When he did take flight, he sent me a beautiful "chirp, chirp" thank-you.

It was a magical moment. The red-tailed hawk is a messenger, and it shows up when we begin to move toward our soul purpose more dynamically. When the bird appeared in my life in such a beautiful and dynamic way, I knew that I was fully on my path. It was a powerful gift to be able to hold the hawk in my hands and feel his life energy. The red-tailed hawk has remained a reminder of my own power and connection to Spirit to this day.

Animal-spirit totems are conscious spiritual energies that choose us, not the other way around. Just as the living relationships between us and our companion animals are chosen by them, so does the spirit of the animal choose our spiritual-totem relationships.

The Wisdom Gifts of Seven Sacred Sign-Bearers

There are seven levels of totems that correspond to the same life themes as the seven chakras: survival/physical, sexuality/procreation, ego-self/individuation, community/love, communication/creativity, intuition/vision, and thought/spirituality.

1. The **first totem animal** aligns with your physical identity, your health, your body in general, your physical dwelling places, and your material experience with money. This sacred sign-bearer is the guardian of family, ancestral spirits, survival needs, and the basic right to be here. The corresponding element is earth. The color is red. The shadow element (or negative aspect) is fear.

2. The **second totem animal** aligns with your emotional

identity, your feelings, your sexuality, and your ability to express emotions in general. This sacred sign-bearer is the guardian of your interpersonal relationships, your partnerships, the capacity to feel pleasure, and the right to feel and desire. The corresponding element is water. The color is orange. The shadow element is guilt.

3. The **third totem animal** aligns with your ego-self, sense of purpose, self-worth, self-esteem, and capacity for healthy individuation. This sacred sign-bearer is the guardian of your physical solar plexus, your personal sense of identity, self-definition, autonomy, individuality, and how you see yourself in the world. It's the guardian of the correct use of personal power and authority and the right to act and be an individual. The corresponding element is fire. The color is yellow. The shadow element is shame.

4. The **fourth totem animal** aligns with your heart and your ability to give and receive love, to love yourself, to be empathetic, to know compassion, and to be caring and sensitive to others' needs. It also helps you remain in balance when in community with others. This sacred sign-bearer is the guardian of your heart center; your love relationships; and your capacity for devotion, kindness, and altruism. It's the guardian of your basic right to love and be loved. The corresponding element is air. The color is green. The shadow element is grief.

5. The **fifth totem animal** aligns with your ability to communicate; and with self-expression, creativity, and speaking your truth in the world. This sacred sign-bearer is the guardian of your voice and physical throat, your capacity to tell the truth, and your ability to think symbolically. It's the guardian of your basic right to hear the truth, as well as speak it. The corresponding element is sound. The color is blue. The shadow element is the lie.

6. The **sixth totem animal** aligns with your third eye and your ability to perceive patterns, to dream, to visualize, and to imagine.

This sacred sign-bearer is the guardian of intuition and all psychic gifts, memories, and dream states. It's the guardian of your basic right to perceive and see beyond the physical world. The corresponding element is light. The color is purple. The shadow element is illusion/delusion.

7. The **seventh totem animal** aligns with your crown center—the link between the mortal incarnate self, the soul, and Spirit. It aligns with your capacity for thoughtfulness, analysis, broad understanding, and most important, the sense of spiritual connectivity. It helps the experience of the immanent soul and the mystical, transcendent revelation of Divinity, Higher Power, *I Am* Presence, Cosmic Consciousness, and so forth. This sacred sign-bearer is the guardian of your personal soul, your inner witness, and the pathway to Spirit. It's the guardian of your basic right to know, to learn, and to express your spirituality. The corresponding element is thought. The color is white. The shadow element is attachment/obsession.

There are many ways to invite your animal totems to reveal themselves to you. I've developed an effective visioning exercise that will show you which one has come to help you with the different aspects of your life. This exercise is meant to be done three times on separate occasions (do *not* do them all on the same day) because there are three separate ways to understand the power of the sign-bearers and how they play out in your life.

The first time, you'll connect with the seven totem animals that adopted you at birth. Invite the spirits of the mammals, birds, insects, or reptiles that are your constant powers for this lifetime. These are your personal sacred sign-bearers.

The second time, you'll connect with the seven temporary helpers that are currently working with you. These animal totems are with you now, offering their guidance, empowerment, and wisdom. They may be temporary powers that have come in to help the birth totems aid you on your current experience of life. These are your helper sacred sign-bearers.

The third time, you'll connect to the ones that have come to help with your shadow—the negative aspects of your mortal self that keep you separate from Spirit. These animals are important totems to help give you strength to heal your wounded ego. They'll help you face your fears and the wounds within you that need healing and that prevent success and authenticity in your life. They're the sacred sign-bearers that will show you what you lack and which of their archetypal powers you need to call upon in order to heal.

Before you begin, go through the Guide to Sacred Sign-Bearers (Chapter 17) and read all the descriptions of land, air, and water creatures one time to allow your consciousness to awaken and ignite the connections to the animals.

Meet Your Totems

Now it's time to settle in for meditation. You can use my CD *Journey Through the Chakras* to invite your totem animals to reveal themselves to you, or follow the instructions below using your favorite meditation music. Just make sure you're in a comfortable place where you can relax undisturbed for 30 to 45 minutes. Most important, have your journal beside you to write down the details of your experiences.

1. Imagine you're in the beautiful sanctuary of an ancient forest glen and you can hear the wind rustling in the trees. The ocean is nearby, and you can hear the waves gently lapping along the shore.

2. Make yourself comfortable in your vision. Perhaps you're resting on a soft, mossy spot at the base of an old, wise tree or sitting in a crystal that's been worn into the shape of a comfy chair. Let your imagination create the environment.

3. Visualize the color red swirling all around you, and ask your first animal totem to reveal itself. It will appear, coming out of the red sparkling light. Let your totem choose you, and thank it for coming with a blessing of love. Spend some time feeling the connection between you.

4. Once you've met that totem, do exactly the same process with the colors orange, yellow, green, blue, violet, and white.

After you've been through these seven colors, you'll have a list of seven animals. When you do this exercise on subsequent days to meet your current helpers and shadow helpers, you'll likely find that some of them repeat. It's rare to have 21 different totems, but it's possible (although it might be a tad crowded!).

It's important to acknowledge your sacred sign-bearers. Offer each one a prayer of gratitude in acceptance of its wisdom gifts after you've pondered its presence in your life. Take time to get to know your totems, studying and learning about their spiritual significance as much as you can. The guide in Chapter 17 is a starting point, plus the animals will reveal other gifts to you through meditation. There's also reference material and suggested reading at the end of this book.

Once you have your seven animal totems identified for each category, see how they get along with each other. Are any threatening to the others? If so, this shows which areas in your life are weak and need strengthening and which ones may be too dominant. You can meditate and ask for help from another animal totem or build a bridge of truce between the more difficult ones.

You should find this process a fun way to get to know yourself, heal old negative patterns, and connect to deep archetypal wisdom and power you may not have known before. Just remember to keep an open mind and let the animals guide you on your quest to know your purpose, your destiny, and the choices that will reveal themselves to you on your journey. The language of oracles, omens, and signs is fluid and steeped in symbolism and metaphor. Its territory is vast, yet it's made accessible through Spirit, using Nature to guide you (and all of us) deeper into beauty and Light.

As famed anthropologist and sociologist J. J. Bachofen said, "The symbol strikes its roots in the most secret depths of the soul; language skims over the surface of the understanding like a soft breeze. . . . Words make the infinite finite, symbols carry the spirit beyond the finite world of becoming into the realm of infinite being."

CHAPTER 12

IT'S A BATH;
IT'S A CLOUD;
IT'S A MESSAGE!

This story actually begins in the tub, after an inspiring and intriguing visit with my dear friend Kim White. As well as being one of the most accurate psychics I know (besides me), she's an expert in herbal magic, and she gave me some packets of herbs to put in my bath. There were perhaps 300 different types of herbs with various healing properties included in the tiny packets. I'd never smelled such rich natural scents. She had a giant bag of the mixture, and holding it made me feel as if Nature herself was touching my soul. Kim said to place the herbs in the bath and pray to them for guidance.

Knowing that Spirit is in all Life—and was most definitely present in these herbs—I had no trouble asking for guidance to be sent to me through this medium. I swirled the herbs around the water, asking for a sign about what would be in store for me on my next trip. Marc and I were leaving the following weekend to go to Las Vegas for the Hay House I Can Do It! conference, and then we were driving to Sedona, Arizona, to decide if it would be the right place for us to spend the winter.

My senses opened up, and as I connected to my oracular consciousness, I began to see symbols appear in the bath. I saw a number of dancing figures begin to form in the water, and I saw that as a positive image of community. The herbs "felt" friendly.

Kim told me to take the herbal bath every night for three nights, so I did. The same dancing figures appeared in the water each time, as if the herbs had a personality and were being playful with me. We traveled to Las Vegas a few days later, leaving the herbs behind, and we had a great time as we always do at every Hay House event.

When we got to Sedona, we were fortunate to connect with First Class Charter and Tours, a wonderful company that arranges all sorts of tours and spiritually based experiential excursions. They introduced us to a number of fascinating individuals, including a Peruvian shaman named Wachan Bajiyoperak who was living in the area and facilitating sacred ceremonies.

Meeting him left a lasting impression on me. A deeply spiritual man, he exuded the kind of wise knowing, humility, and calm friendliness that can only come from someone truly secure in his own shoes. When he told us the literal meaning of his name, "Deer of Light," I was sure we had met someone special, as he embodied his name with an undeniable sacred energy and respect—a true gentle, noble spirit. We immediately liked him.

After a short prayer to set our intentions, the three of us drove off into the early sun. He took us to the red rocks for a traditional shamanic ceremony to ask the Spirit of the land if we might be welcome there.

The most important part of this story happened when we were on the cliff side of a place called Airport Vortex. In accordance with Wachan's guidance, we meditated and offered corn and tobacco to the rocks, and then found a place where we decided to lie down and contemplate the energy surrounding us. While this was happening, I felt the grounding energies of the red rocks pull me inward. It felt really good, especially because as an intuitive I can easily become disconnected from the earth if I'm not careful.

The sky was bright blue and crisp, as it is in Arizona at 7 A.M. in May. With my eyes closed, I knew that a cloud was passing over the sun because my eyelids became dark. I also had a sense of a cool rain, although that wasn't going to happen anytime soon. Then I opened my eyes and saw the same shapes of dancing figures that had appeared in my bathtub, swirling with Kim's magic herbal mixture—but this time they were in a formation of clouds.

They were identical, as if Spirit was drawing me a picture in the sky. The figures even moved in the same direction and dissolved in the same way. I knew they were a sign that this place would be important to me. When we were leaving, I intuitively knew that we should offer the red rocks the gift of water—it's almost as if the rocks said they were thirsty. We'd asked the land if we would be welcome, and the clouds were the answer for us.

Signs from Above

This is a story that sounds amazing in our modern context, but it would have been commonplace in ancient times. The divination method of asking for and receiving messages through cloud formations has a formal name: *aeromancy*. It also refers to any atmospheric phenomena such as storms, wind, comets, stars, rainbows, rings around the moon, or other natural forces that affect the appearance of the sky.

The most famous example in Christian mythology is the appearance of the star of Bethlehem, heralding the birth of Jesus. In A.D. 1066, King Harold II was told that the appearance of the shooting star across the sky was a bad omen for England, while William the Conqueror was told what we now know as Halley's Comet would ensure his victory. The battle of Hastings was indeed won by William, and England was defeated.

A more common reference to aeromancy occurs when we see rainbows. Everyone knows a rainbow means good fortune after difficulty, right? Some of us even believe that magical little people hide their pots of gold at the rainbow's end. This comes from the ancient divination practice of aeromancy joined with a belief in nature spirits called devas and leprechauns.

Still, there's something that exists beyond the superstitions created as a result of weather conditions. Who doesn't expect some damage in a terrible storm? Is that the wild behavior of Nature acting on her own? Or is it a response to our poor stewardship of Earth? Many of us do believe the signs around us now are a result of our mistreatment of the planet—perhaps it's a general protest directed at all of us. Nonetheless, there's a form of interactive, personal, intimate dialogue that's possible, linking our tiny selves to the vast sky and our consciousness to that of Spirit. And it's the clouds that best answer our questions.

So if you want to cultivate a relationship with Spirit through the medium of clouds, here's a fun exercise to develop the dialogue. Remember, though, that seeing the images is easy—interpreting them and discerning what's pertinent or not is the work you're required to do. And as with everything, you get better with practice.

How to Read the Clouds

Make yourself comfortable somewhere in nature (such as in a park or at the beach) or in a seat next to a window with an unobstructed view of the sky. If you live in a city where natural surroundings aren't available, this can work by watching the cloud formations reflecting on a building (preferably one with lots of glass). You'll need about 30 minutes to relax and allow the images to speak to you.

Begin with a breathing meditation, inhaling through your nose and exhaling through your mouth as if your breath is forming a circle. Just concentrate on that for a few minutes until you feel relaxed.

Now think of some guidance you need in any area of your life. The first thing that speaks to you intuitively is the correct area.

Allow yourself to open like a flower—imagine your five senses unfolding and amplifying. Connect to your oracular consciousness by allowing your imagination to merge with your intuition. (This feels obvious, even though it's subtle.)

Look at the clouds and see what images "pop" out at you. Write them down as you see them, and don't worry about interpreting them until you've spent a few minutes allowing the shapes to reveal themselves to you.

In closing, say a prayer of gratitude to the Divine, to Spirit for listening.

Then, taking one image at a time, refer to the Guide to the Sacred Sign-Bearers (Chapter 17). This gives you a starting point for contemplation. The traditional interpretations may be augmented by any other personal symbolism. You should find that the images tell a story. You'll be able to confirm the details and how accurate your interpretation was in hindsight.

You'll find answers—and sometimes more questions—that will make you look into the deeper meaning of things. Sometimes Spirit's messages will be playful, and other times they'll be deep and profound.

Then there are periods when you won't make a connection at all. End those sessions the same way—by thanking the Divine for listening to your request for guidance. It's likely that you're meant to receive another sign altogether, which may come in a dream, by receiving a Cledon, or by having a flash of insight where your inner voice will lead you to the answer—but not necessarily when you want it. No one can force Spirit to respond according to any particular schedule. Guidance always comes if you're sincerely asking for it, but on Spirit's timetable.

Sometimes, however, the sign is quite straightforward. Here's one of my favorite anecdotes illustrating this; it's by Sister Joanne Morgan from Ontario, Canada.

Cosmic Kisses

I felt called to do something extraordinary with my life and sought a connection to Something/Someone bigger than myself. This led to me becoming a nun in a Catholic International Missionary Congregation, which took me on a journey to Peru, Rome, and beyond. (I now live in Canada.)

These experiences have marked me in so many ways and strengthened my connection to Spirit. For instance, when I was visiting our Sisters in Myanmar, I asked to go to the Buddhist monastery to spend the day with a Buddhist nun. It was like a homecoming, with an energy that felt so familiar. The synchronicity of this meeting led me to discover a few years later that Buddha is one of my Spirit guides.

I've experienced Spirit's messages coming to me in many different ways. Once, I was on a private retreat in Winnipeg. Spirit became the skywriter through cloud formations in the ever-expansive prairie skies. The last day of the retreat, after coming home from a walk, I looked up in the sky and there— right above my apartment—were two huge double X's or spiritual kisses. Indeed, it was a double confirmation and blessing of Divine love.

We started this chapter in the bathtub, so let's end it there, too, with a relaxing and effective oracle tool.

There's an Oracle in My Tub?

You think I'm kidding, right? Well, try it, and you'll see what an accurate reflection you'll find in your bathwater. You can create a water oracle and ask for a vision, and Spirit will pay you a visit right in the tub.

I always make jokes about how outdoorsy I'm *not*, even though I'm all about Nature. At my age, I'd rather not do a "vision quest" out in the wilderness by myself like my friend Denise Linn (the author and spiritual teacher) does. My most comfortable idea of such a search for the Divine is sitting in the tub, surrounded by candles and meditating on the shapes forming in the water around me. This is one of my favorite ways of connecting to Spirit. It originates from an ancient Greek divination tradition called *hydromancy,* which originally meant to study signs reflected in the sea or any other natural body of water, and also patterns in rain or the ripples made by throwing a stone into still water.

How to Create a Bath Oracle

You'll need:

1. Four candles, one for each corner of the tub, symbolically identifying the elements of water, air, earth, and fire

2. A cup of Epsom salts

3. A small amount of bubble bath

4. A small handful of any product called a "milk bath"

Fill the tub, putting in all the bath additives, and then swirl the mixture with your hand. The reason you need all these ingredients is to create a milky, foamy surface instead of mountains of bubbles (that can work, too, although it's a little more complicated to discern the patterns). Oil also works, but you need to cut it with something like Epsom salts to act as a dispersant.

While swirling the bathwater, say a personal prayer to Spirit and ask for a vision to show you what you need to know on your path, for the highest good of all. Next, light the candles; if you don't have room for them around the tub, place them on the sink or somewhere else to signify that the ritual has begun. Then enter the bath.

As you soak, swirl the water three times and watch the patterns on the surface begin to form. This will take approximately 15 minutes or so. Pay attention to the symbols and how they play out in your day.

I did this exercise today after I came back from the chiropractor. I was really grumpy because I knew I still had a lot more work to do on my book, and I was feeling overwhelmed. I hadn't slept and needed to meditate—but I could only think, *Work, work, work!*

As I settled into the tub, I began to notice all these figures of otters swirling around in front of me. Well, of course! Otters were reminding me to be playful and not take myself so seriously. Then I noticed the shape of a cat turning a somersault around what looked like a television set. Yes! I needed to set a boundary with someone who was bombarding me with e-mail. I'd been putting it off, and I knew immediately that this was the message. Then the foam formed a giant tree: It was time to get grounded and trust in the natural process. My grounding meditation (which is a free download on my Website's Member's Lounge) is all about connecting to the wisdom energy of a tree.

After my bath, I did the grounding exercise and felt a thousand times better. Spirit wanted me to have some fun after I did something I'd been putting off. All I needed to remember was to stay grounded. All would be well. In fact, all *is* well.

CHAPTER 13

11:11—SIGNS AND ANGELS

For as long as I can remember, 11:11 has showed up when I need confirmation that I'm on the right track, to make me pay attention, and to help me be alert to my surroundings and events. I've always considered the appearance of this double number to be profound and meaningful, as if Spirit was making itself known in my life and cared about my welfare.

I noticed it a lot when I was a kid but only had a curious "tickle" about it. One incident, however, remains indelibly etched in my memory. When I was five years old, I learned a very important lesson through these numbers.

My parents forbade me to cross the street alone, so I was isolated on the wrong side of the road from the candy store. My little "friend" Marky taunted me from his rich kingdom across the street, waving his yummy treats after his daily trip to the store. One day, I was in my room and the doorbell rang just as I glanced at my little white clock with angels on it. It was exactly 11:11. (The clock was one of the early "digital" mechanical types where the numbers rolled down as the time changed.)

Marky was at the door. He asked me in a conspiratorial tone if I'd like to pay him to go to the store to buy me candy. As I was hostage to my parents' financial support, this would only be possible if I stole a quarter.

I promptly decided that God would forgive my theft because it was for candy, which was a very good cause. When I went into my parents' room to take the coin, I noticed that their mahogany clock also said 11:11. The other weird thing is, I remember that clock starting to chime faintly just as I began to think that stealing wasn't such a good idea. But my conflicted five-year-old self began to salivate, and I made my first bad decision.

The next thing I knew, my pal—silver in hand—started screaming for my dad to tell him that I stole a quarter. Needless to say, I was spanked and sent to my room. As I sat whimpering, sugarless and betrayed, I noticed something odd: My clock *still* said 11:11.

I remember this because it was also the first moment in my life I recall feeling shame and betrayal. Today, I'd interpret the numbers as a warning to stay on track. The clock in my parents' room had chimed when I was about to choose between right and wrong.

The other interesting thing to note is the way I experienced the numbers—it was as if they were asking me to look at them. Why would I be interested in the position of the hands on a clock in my parents' room? I was five years old and fixated on candy. There was an unmistakable moment of awareness that was "other."

Throughout my teen years when I was in relative stages of distress and angst—and always around the times of prescient dreams or strong intuitive intrusions—I saw 11:11 (or just 11) frequently. It showed up on soup labels, clocks, locker numbers, and expiration dates on bags of cookies. I would even be the 11th person to be picked for a team in gym.

When my girlfriend asked me to go home with her one night when we were at a bar, 11:11 was the number on the clock. That was 11:11 letting me know that going home was the right choice; I'd be protected. But I turned away with my drink in hand and remained till the bar closed. That's when I accepted a ride from some local guys, which led to my being raped later that evening.

I told this story in my first book, *Remembering the Future,* and it's unnecessary to repeat the entire tale here. However, it's interesting to note that experiencing this violence was the pivotal moment that led to a huge awakening of my clairvoyant perception. In moments of reflection, I also believe I saw 11:11 that evening because Spirit was telling me that I'd be okay in the end.

From today's vantage point, I know that that night was the beginning of a dangerous and dark initiation by fire. I can only believe that all that I *was* had to be burned away so that I could one day rise up again from the ashes like a phoenix. I've come to believe that out of suffering comes the invitation to wisdom. Had I not experienced so much, perhaps I wouldn't be such an effective intuitive today.

The number 11:11 then faded in and out of memory as I began my descent into escapism, addiction, and self-denial. The next nine years were filled with extreme experiences, and I unconsciously courted the violations I'd come to accept as my personal legacy. When I hit bottom at 27, after trying unsuccessfully to stop drinking and using drugs on my own, I had the most extreme moment of surrender.

The last morning of that life began like any other. I emerged from a drug dealer's basement as usual—strung out, confused, and scared, having said and done unthinkable things. I hated myself, my failures, my lies, and my lost life. I was hurting myself, and those around me were shameful casualties in my wake. I hated my life, but I couldn't stop any of it. I was powerless, and I was dying.

I was so terribly tired. That particular morning, I screamed silently inside one last time, and I surrendered completely when I said, "God, help me." Then I had another life-altering moment.

The story I tell now isn't about the absolute sense of a guardian spirit behind me, shimmering in a gossamer shadow. Nor is it about the fact that I knew I'd never have to go back there again (to the drug dealer's basement or the place of despair and self-injury), nor that I sensed I'd gone through some kind of initiation or trial by fire. Looking back, all of those things are absolutely true, but the story is really about the cab ride home.

The driver stopped at my door after being stuck in early-morning rush-hour traffic. Everything felt surreal. I saw my mother's worried face peering from behind the drapes in her bedroom window. I remember that the fare was $12.40, but I had exactly $11.11. The driver accepted the money and said, " I guess this will be your last stop." He was right—11:11 became my true friend from that day on.

Coincidence? I Think Not.

I'm not the only one for whom this figure has special significance. I received hundreds of e-mails when I asked for 11:11 stories on my weekly radio show on **HayHouseRadio.com**® and on my Website. Why is it that so many people see these specific double numbers often enough that coincidence just isn't a possible explanation?

I had a reading with numerology expert Tania Gabrielle, who's now a frequent guest on my radio show. I was astounded by the depth, accuracy, and detail of her extraordinary insight into my life. We spoke of the 11:11 phenomenon, and she told me that she'd run across many people who had this recurrence.

She has her own understanding of what this might mean. She told me that when the first great spiritual/linguistic minds created alphabets, each letter was thought to convey a set of basic qualities or energies. And each one could be represented by a number.

Bearing this in mind, this is how Tania identifies these qualities in the English alphabet:

Number 1 resonates to confidence, inventiveness, leadership, action, and creative thought. Letters corresponding to 1 are A, J, and S.

Number 2 vibrates to cooperation, diplomacy, balance, partnership, graciousness, sensitivity, and peace. Number 2 letters are B, K, and T.

Number 3 is about inspiration, self-expression, creative talent, the gift of words, the gift of vision, artistic gifts, prophecy, and joy. Letters corresponding to 3 are C, L, and U.

Number 4 resonates with a strong foundation, practicality, determination, discipline, organization, being a good worker, and loving family. Its corresponding letters are D, M, and V.

Number 5 vibrates to change, adventure, freedom, and versatility and is resourceful, energetic, and curious. Number 5 letters are E, N, and W.

Number 6 is humanitarian, nurturing, artistic, domestic, and a teacher. Letters corresponding to 6 are F, O, and X.

Number 7 is the vibration of silence, spirituality, scientific studies, analysis, observation, meditation, and the occult. The letters for 7 are G, P, and Y.

Number 8 resonates with power, strength, abundance, authority, infinity, business, and a balance of energies. Letters corresponding to 8 are H, Q, and Z.

Number 9 describes love, brotherhood, compassion, philanthropy, artistic gifts, and leadership. Its letters are I and R.

Every letter was assigned a number simply by taking the position it holds in the alphabet and adding the digits together to create its root number. For example, the letter *L* is the 12th letter, and 1 + 2 = 3, which is its root number. Words can be reduced in a similar way.

The exception to this formula is a special category of double-digit *master numbers*—11, 22, 33, 44, and so on. Of these, 11 is extra special.

The name Jesus resonates to 11: J/1 E/5 S/1 U/3 S/1. Light is also an 11 vibration. Other 11 words are *enlightenment, mastery, creative, vibration,* and *psychic.* In the Kabbalah, the letter *O* can be counted as either a 6 or a zero. Looking at the word *God,* where *O* is zero, God also totals 11.

The figure 11:11 is a symbol of the path to the wisdom of Spirit, which is always opened through this door. It confirms our eternal connection to the Divine and invites us to pay attention to the synchronicities in our lives. Even the difficult experiences I've had marked by 11:11 carry profound lessons that have served to push my awareness to include a greater vista of life. The double number is the double signal for the Divine.

It's no wonder then that 11:11 is popping up with greater frequency, confirming the constant presence of God. This phenomenon is a signal, letting you know you're on the right track. In a very real sense, when you see these numbers, Spirit is speaking directly to you. It's reminding you, *Body, mind, and spirit, you are one with Me.*

Your Journal of 11:11 (and other Recurring Numbers)

Keep a record of the times you see the number 11 or the double figure 11:11.

1. Write down what you were doing when this experience happened.

2. How many times in your history did something important happen around the time you received a nudge from Spirit through 11:11?

3. What kind of intuitive feelings did you have?

4. How do you now recognize this as a message from Spirit?

5. What does it mean to you to know that Spirit is communicating with you through these numbers?

6. What are some of the other recurring numbers common to your experience?

7. What kind of events do you relate these to?

8. Can you track patterns through the recurring numbers? If so, what are they, and what can you learn about yourself through them?

Here's a quick and synchronistic story to finish up the 11:11 connection. At the time my lease was up on my Jeep, I really wanted to get a hybrid car. I was frustrated, though, because of the long wait for them and the high prices in Canada. I was given an opportunity to lease another car for a shorter period, while I waited for the new environmentally friendly vehicles to be more accessible the next year. I was unsure of what to do because I really wanted to get a hybrid right away, but the one that was available was way too expensive for my budget. So I prayed for a sign from Spirit to help show me the next right action.

To make a long story short, the salesman then showed me a beautiful new Dodge with exactly 11 miles on it. The first four numbers of the vehicle registration number were 11:11. I took the car. I forgot to mention that my personal number is 11, too.

Finding Your Personal Sacred Numbers

Everyone has a special personal resonance with different numbers. They show you specific themes that will play out in your life as you journey from birth to crossing over. They demonstrate how your life has a unique purpose, what you'll be inspired by, what you'll be attracted to, and what strengths and challenges may be inherent to your personality and soul. You can find out about your life purpose and your destiny through the numbers assigned to you on your birth date and by your full given name.

The Number of Your Life Purpose

The purpose of your life—what you're here to do—can be found by adding the numerals of your birth date. The life-purpose number is the root number of the total. So add them up like this:

- Say your birthday is October 16, 1957 (10/16/1957)
- You'll add 1+0+1+6+1+9+5+7 = 30
- Determine the root number of 30: 3+0 = 3

Remember, the number 3 is about inspiration, self-expression, creative talent, gift of words, gift of vision, artistic gifts, prophecy, and joy. Letters corresponding to 3 are C, L, and U.

So your life purpose will be to express yourself in service to humankind through the attributes listed above. You may find yourself to be a writer, painter, musician, or teacher. At the very least, you'll feel whole by surrounding yourself with these qualities in your hobbies.

The Number of Your Destiny

To find out your destiny number and the reason why you're actually here, add up the numbers corresponding to all the letters of the name you were given at birth.

Use this chart to help you:

1	2	3	4	5	6	7	8	9
A	B	C	D	E	F	G	H	I
J	K	L	M	N	O	P	Q	R
S	T	U	V	W	X	Y	Z	

- Take the name Jan Mary Doe
- J+A+N+M+A+R+Y+D+O+E is 1+1+5+4+1+9+7+4+6+5 = 43
- 4+3 = 7

Number 7 is the vibration of silence, spirituality, scientific studies, analysis, observation, meditation, and the occult. The corresponding letters are G, P, and Y.

So this person is here to learn about life through the vibration of 7, which also means grace, refinement of ideas, philosophy, deep thought, and illuminating what is hidden. This is the loner number as well; people with this vibration often prefer their own company.

The Life-Purpose and Destiny-Numbers Guide

Adding to Tania's general list, here's a more detailed idea of how numbers relate to you in a more personal way if they're your life-purpose or destiny numbers.

Number 1: Your lesson is to learn self-reliance, independence, and leadership. You'll acquire personal accountability and responsibility. You dislike authority and are best suited to be at the front of the line, so to speak. You're brilliant at beginning new projects and have the capacity for great success when you have the opportunity for advancement.

Number 2: Your lesson is to succeed though partnerships. You have a great sensitivity to others' needs and make a compassionate healer. You'll learn through relationships and teach others by example. Harmony is something you crave; and you're naturally a peacekeeper, mediator, and diplomat. You'll be happiest in a relationship.

Number 3: You're here to communicate and create! You're naturally optimistic and love to spread that attitude around. You're unhappy with constraints and need to be stimulated and allowed to be creative. You're blessed with ingenuity, imagination, and vision. Others enjoy having you around. Your lesson is to express yourself in as many ways as possible.

Number 4: You're very practical; and your lesson is to experience your world in an ordered, organized way—and to help others do the same. You have patience and excellent managerial skills, and are loyal and committed. Your success will come through work and organizing others. Disciplined and honest, you're trustworthy and people admire your sense of responsibility.

Number 5: You're social, flirtatious, enthusiastic, and charismatic. Your lesson is to explore learning through varied experiences. Travel is important because you gain understanding of your life by being exposed to new environments and experiences. You love people and tend to be very popular. You have to watch being bored and are suited to do various things throughout your journey.

Number 6: Home, family, friendships, babies, pets, and tending to others are the ways you'll explore in this lifetime. Your lesson is to nurture and to experience life through love and parenting others. You're the natural healer and will be drawn to that art. You're at your best around beauty and comfort. Your affection and generosity of spirit in love and friendship makes the world a happier place.

Number 7: Your lesson is to explore the world philosophically and analytically. Your experience is one of dignity and honor. The more knowledge you have, the happier you are. You love to spend time on your own, and you need to respect the people you're with. Books are important to you, and you love nature. Your success comes with imparting knowledge to others.

Number 8: A unique problem solver, you'll find your lesson is to explore the world of manifesting. You're very good with money and turning ideas into successful businesses. You're here to succeed through ambition and are best suited to head up large organizations that wield socioeconomic power. Your happiness comes when you learn to balance material pursuits with the spiritual.

Number 9: Your lesson is to help the collective raise their vibration through imparting wisdom brought from previous lifetimes. You're passionate, romantic, wise beyond personal experience, idealistic, and understanding. You're a humanitarian and are happiest giving to others; you have a desire to support and elevate others. You're empathetic and deeply in tune with how others think. You love well, and it's likely that you're well loved in return.

Master Numbers

This is when we don't reduce the double numbers down to their root. For example, 11 remains the same—we don't then reduce, 1+1= 2. As I mentioned, these double numbers are called master numbers and denote a special purpose, sometimes with great responsibility, for those whose personal number is 11, 22, 33, or 44. Their life experiences tend to be extreme, with highs, lows, and many difficult challenges to make them ready to express themselves with the highest vibration inherent in the master number.

- My birthday is July 17, 1958
- Add 7+1+7+1+9+5+8= 38
- 3+8 = 11

There's that 11 again!

Number 11 is sometimes known as the *Master Psychic.* It generally denotes someone who's here for a greater spiritual purpose or who will be concerned with spiritual or theological pursuits. It shows the highest capacity for intuition and relating to the

Unseen. It also indicates a person who will be involved in music (the root number of music is also 11) and other artistic pursuits. As an intuitive and musical recording artist, I can see how this easily applies to the flow of my life.

Number 22 is known as the *Master Builder.* People who resonate to this number are highly sensitive to their physical and emotional surroundings. They're masters of detail and capable of building anything, bringing the inspiration of the 11 vibration into the material realm. Usually very successful at manifesting anything, they may become society's benefactors, creating financial foundations to help the concrete workings of necessities like bridges, roads, and other structures.

Number 33 is known as the *Master Giver.* Selfless humanitarians, these people will be in the forefront of caring for others. They're motivated by compassion and fairness. They also have the capacity for deep spiritual wisdom, although few ever reach this potential. This is the number of the humanitarian savior, of service, and of responsibility.

Number 44 is known as the *Master Healer.* This number is about the commitment to heal, and help solve problems for others. It's about leadership, strength of conviction, and inner strength. This is also a very practical number. Houdini was a 44, and he was able to solve the most amazing and seemingly impossible dilemmas. These folks are very resourceful and can find unusual ways to help others. Edgar Cayce (also a 44) was able to diagnose, treat, and heal patients while in a trance. The words *therapist* and *minister* resonate to the number 44.

There are other master numbers, but these four are the most common ones for birth dates and names. Numbers such as 55, 66, 77, 88, and 99 will usually only be found as the root numbers of other words.

Knowing your life-purpose and destiny numbers is always helpful because they're your anchor points on your life's journey. They're within you and will remain as constants, regardless of how your outer life changes and progresses. If you want to delve into this subject further, refer to the resources in the Bibliography at the end of this book.

For now, pay close attention to the patterns of numbers that appear regularly in your life. Within their sequence may be an important message from Spirit!

Clearly, many people are nudged by numbers, receiving messages from Spirit. This often happens when 11:11 appears and Spirit whispers, "Remember the All is in the Small . . . body, mind, and soul. You are one with Me."

CHAPTER 14

YOU SAY FORTUNE COOKIE; I SAY *ALEUROMANCY*

One of the things I look forward to when ordering Chinese food is the fortune cookie—you know the little ritual at the end of the meal when everybody sits around and asks, "What did you get?" "What does yours say?" And then you laugh at how ridiculous the sayings are. But every once in a while, people get a message that says something pertinent about their lives and are struck by the synchronicity.

Even though I always thought fortune cookies were silly, intuitively I knew that somewhere in Chinese history these things must have meant something. It's true that many sacred traditions are diluted and distorted over time, and some are borrowed and given new appearances and names to suit their new proprietors. I assumed the same thing happened with the fortune cookie.

The only problem with researching the great sacred traditions of Divine dialogue in Asia is that you won't find the origins of the fortune cookie anywhere—it's actually an American invention. But if you look to ancient Greece, you'll find its true ancestor.

Aleuromancy, which means "divination by flour" in Greek, is the true name of this tradition of using baked goods as a vehicle for Spirit messages. So all you bakers, let me show you how to create a most exciting and accurate oracle tool.

First, I'll share a little history. As with the Delphic oracle, Apollo was considered to be the illuminating power behind this practice. The ancient Greeks wrote symbols on pieces of cloth or papyrus and then rolled them in dough that had been mixed nine times, placing the dough in the fire to be baked. Once they were cooked, the dough balls were put on a tray and passed around to a group of people who came together to ask a question of the Divine. (Many oracle experiences in ancient times were social events.)

The difference between our modern cookie messages such as "You will be lucky today" or "Eat too much cookie and get large behind" and the Greek's messages are obvious. The ancient flour oracles were filled with messages where the symbols were sacred. Ceremony and ritual were involved, as well as invoking the god Apollo. The messages were philosophical in nature and pertained to different life experiences. They were used as a means to discern the will of the Divine in answer to a particular question. All in all, it was a little more serious than chomping on egg rolls and then breaking open the cookies to laugh at the fortunes.

Important decisions were made based on the messages received from the flour oracles of ancient times. Additionally, guidance was sought from the markings inside the bowl where the leftover flour-and-water mixture—the ancient cookie dough—remained.

There was a higher intentional consciousness invoked in the whole experience from beginning to end. And you can have an enlightening and fun time today, using this oracle in the way it was originally intended.

The Sacred Treasure Oracle

I've created my own version of the flour oracle based on the essential movement of 27 archetypes of the human experience as it unfolds from birth to death. (You'll learn about these Universal Unfoldments in Chapter 16.) These archetypes are found in most wisdom teachings and are represented in such complicated divination systems as the Tarot. This is a fun way to track your progress on the ever-evolving journey through life, and it makes a great gift, too!

You'll need to mix basic cookie dough in a large white bowl using a wooden spoon. The white bowl signifies the purity of Spirit, and the wooden spoon connects the process to the natural world. The ingredients you must use are:

1. Flour, to represent the power of the earth and to give manifest form

2. Sugar or honey, to represent the sweetness of life

3. Water, to represent the ebb and flow of life

4. Fire (stove), to represent the activity and creativity inherent in all things

5. Salt, to preserve and to represent the infinite soul

6. Butter, to represent abundance

7. Milk, to represent nourishment

8. Eggs, to represent the foundations of birth

You can use any combination of these ingredients in any cookie recipe you enjoy, since the idea is to eat them after you bake them. They have to be plain, though—no chocolate chips or raisins since those will dilute the power invoked in the ritual. Make sure you have enough dough to form 27 cookies.

(If you're not planning to eat the cookies, make a basic dough using 3 cups flour, 1 cup sugar, ½ cup water, ½ teaspoon salt, ¼ pound softened butter, ½ cup milk, and 4 eggs. Mix it all together in the white bowl. This will give you enough for two batches of Sacred Treasure Balls.)

On 27 small pieces of parchment paper (which you can find by the aluminum foil and waxed paper at the grocery store), write or create symbols for the Universal Unfoldments (see Chapter 16). Roll the pieces of paper into tight cylinders.

Make 27 balls from the dough, flatten them a bit, and put one of the paper cylinders on each of them. Roll them up to form the Sacred Treasure Balls. Place them on a cookie sheet (you may have to use a couple of cookie sheets), and bake according to the recipe instructions. (For the basic dough, bake 40 minutes at 325 degrees F. Every oven is different so you may have to play around with this.) Once they've cooled, you can use them for your Sacred Treasure oracle.

Within each of the dough balls is sacred wisdom to illuminate your path as you move forward. The choosing of the cookies will represent your past, your present, and the evolving future of any of seven areas of your life. If you're using this oracle alone, you may ask one question in each of the following seven categories—one per day—over the course of a week. This will give you an overview of all these aspects of your life as they play out through the coming month.

1. Health, physical
2. Community, friends, family
3. Work, job
4. Love relationships, romance
5. Creativity, communication
6. Dreams, ideas
7. Spirituality

If you're choosing to experience this oracle in a group, then each person picks three Sacred Treasure Balls—which represent past influences, the present, and a possible outcome—and then a fourth, representing the catalyst that's accelerating personal growth. You'll need to make two full batches for each group of five people. Because that makes 54 balls, there will be duplicates of the Universal Unfoldments. If you receive the same message twice, it means that this particular experience is amplified in all areas of your life and indicates a transition to a higher consciousness through the portal of the archetype's lessons.

As with all oracle messengers, ask to be shown the will of Spirit for the highest good of all concerned. Also pray for guidance and for the ability to accept the answers that are revealed. Do such a reading no more than once a month. It may take time to fully understand the meanings implied by the symbols and their personal relevance to you, so write it all down and pay attention to what you've learned in hindsight.

Don't Lick the Bowl!

Making these flour oracles will also give you another Spirit message to study: the dough that has settled along the sides of the bowl, which is like the soup oracle. Examine the symbols on the inside of the mixing bowl before you go to sleep. For example, a woman named Kate sent me a story of how she saw a very obvious image of a large dog with specific markings on its hind leg in the bowl—it looked as if it were chasing a ball. A couple months later, through a series of synchronicities, she was led to adopt a shepherd-mix adult dog that had been abandoned by the side of the road with a broken foot. She named him Booboo. When his foot was healed, Booboo's favorite activity was running around the house chasing a ball.

Pay attention to your dreams for the following week, as this bowl will help you bridge the seen and Unseen to retrieve messages from Spirit for the benefit of you and your loved ones. When I was experimenting with this divination technique, I saw four obvious letters in the bowl: *I, Z, G,* and then an *O.* My father's nickname was Zigo! It's not uncommon for symbols to show up pertaining to loved ones who've passed over. But if you don't see anything recognizable after studying it a bit, perhaps Spirit in the cookie dough is just reminding you about the taste of sweetness— so go ahead now and lick the bowl!

CHAPTER 15

STONES THAT SPEAK

Just after my father died, and before I went to live with my friend Beth, I made an appointment to see a healer from New Mexico. He was in town to teach a course on shamanism and see clients. This was an odd and impulsive thing for me to do. I'd seen a bright purple flyer with a phone number and a description of the class and his healings tacked to a telephone pole. I'd been standing in front of a coffee shop waiting for a friend, and it caught my eye as if it were calling to me. I went over, and when I touched it I accidentally pulled it off the pole.

I was in emotional turmoil about what was still unresolved in my heart regarding my parents and my work as an intuitive. I was in a lot of pain because of my dad's death and all the tragedy in my family. At that time, I was beginning to take a strong interest in Native American spirituality, and when I read about this man and his background in anthropology and shamanism, I was very interested in meeting him. Intuitively, I felt that it would be safe and that I needed to know him, so I called and made the appointment.

When I met John Raven for the first time, I was struck by his calm and gentle presence and by his piercing eyes, which were the color of indigo ink. He was a tall and handsome man with long salt-and-pepper hair in a ponytail. His physique was very youthful, but his eyes told me that he must have been in his 70s. He had an otherworldly presence, and I had the strong impression I'd known him before—but of course I never had.

With very little in the way of introduction, he asked me to sit with him quietly, and he began to pray in another language. I suddenly became nervous and fidgety. Then he had me stand while he blew smoke around me and shook a rattle, starting at my feet and moving up and around my head.

I sat back down, transfixed by all of this, while he stared at the smoke in the room. Then he proceeded to tell me everything that was going on in my life in detail, none of which he could have known in advance. It was as if someone had opened me up like a stiff door that needed the hinge oiled; I felt relieved and open.

Then he held out his hand and passed me a small, striated rock that he pulled out of a deerskin bag. He said, "This is a member of the Stone tribe, the oldest among us. This being lives behind what you see, in non-ordinary reality, the Spirit behind the thing. Some people only see an object that is inanimate, a rock made of inorganic material, but those of us who know can see the source of wisdom from the Stone people, living in its memory."

I asked him where he came from, and he told me his heritage was Lakota Sioux. I knew the phrase "all our relations" was attributed to this Native American tribal vision of the human/nature spiritual connectivity. He was showing me how to see this for myself.

John told me to close my eyes, open my heart and mind, pray to the rock, and ask for guidance about my life. I asked him if this was part of the healing, and he said that for me it was. He said I needed to develop a larger worldview that included all of nature as living interdependently with humans. He told me that if I accepted my fate and destiny to be a seer, then I'd need to learn how to see into all of the world and not just some of it. He said very simply that for me to be true in my vision and my capacity to see for others, I'd need to recognize other sources of wisdom in the world besides the human.

I looked closely at the stone and saw images of a cross, a bear, and then a swan. I saw a house and what I thought was a tombstone, followed by the number six. He asked me to tell him what I believed these meant.

Of course, I immediately saw the cross as Christ Consciousness. I was an avid reader of Catherine Ponder and an attendee of Unity Church. I loved to read the Bible as allegory and myth, so I believed that the image of the cross meant that something in me had to die to be reborn, and that it was time to sacrifice some of my old ideas in order to make way for something better.

I knew the bear was about rest—I was tired and needed to regroup and heal. Also, I was studying meditation, and the bear signified that, too. John then told me that the swan was my ability to transform and to see beyond ordinary reality. I asked if the tombstone meant my father's death and he only said, "All life flickers in and out; it's the way of things." With that, he handed me another stone and smiled. It was time to go, and I had a lot to think about.

I met with him a couple more times and had some astounding experiences. He showed me how to connect to the non-ordinary reality that I was already accessing when I did my readings—but it was very different. This was a world beside ours that existed equally; it was populated by all manner of fascinating and incredible spiritual energies that presented themselves to me as living aspects behind the ordinary world. I saw the living vibration of an old weeping willow in a park I walked through to go home. I saw the tree as an old woman who was looking after the ground as if it was her child. I began to notice that the rocks I held had memories and stories to tell. What a gift I'd been given by this man.

When I was supposed to see him for the fourth time, I called to confirm and a woman answered and said that no one by that name was there. I checked the number and asked again, but she said she'd had that number for more than five years and that I was mistaken.

I went to the apartment building where he'd been staying and rang the buzzer. The superintendent happened to come out just then and asked who I was looking for. I told him I was there to see John Raven from New Mexico, and I described him. The super looked at me with mounting suspicion and obvious agitation.

I said that John was also supposed to be holding a workshop in the party room of the building that Saturday. The man looked at me strangely and said that no one fitting John's description was ever there, and there was no party room. The apartment I was ringing was empty and had been for more than a month—ever since an old Native American man who was a chronic alcoholic had died in it.

I was completely freaked out and argued with the super. He just looked spooked and slammed the door in my face muttering, "Crazy, stupid broad. I need a drink."

So were my experiences a dream, or were they real? Did John Raven ever exist? I had so many questions but no answers. When I asked my friends, no one seemed to know what I was talking about either. I knew I'd told a couple of people about my sessions with John, but they claimed I hadn't said anything. Yet the teachings were real, and I wasn't "cuckoo."

I began to study in earnest to learn what I could. I found John's methods congruent with what I discovered in books on shamanism. Yet the entire situation was still puzzling and weird. The number six and the tombstone made sense six months later, however, when my mother was diagnosed with terminal brain cancer and passed away shortly after. Real or dream—or perhaps just two separate realities at a junction that I was meant to cross.

I still remember John Raven's piercing dark eyes and his deep voice telling me, "The stones will speak if you listen to them."

Listening to Stones

This exercise will help you learn how to listen when the Spirit in a stone is speaking to you. First, go to a natural surrounding and set out an intention to find a rock with a message for you; the stone should be the size of a fist or a little larger. Don't try to force it to show itself. The connection is made by subtle energies—you'll be drawn to one if you allow yourself to be "pulled" or "called" to it. It's an intuitive faculty, an amplified "there it is, this must be it" feeling. Once your stone has chosen you, find somewhere to sit and place the rock in front of you, asking for the message to be revealed.

Allow your inner mind to open to your symbolic thought perception or oracular consciousness. It will then begin to discern shapes of insects, birds, animals, faces, numbers, objects, and other shapes. Once you get a clear indication of at least two, spend time interpreting their meanings and how they apply to your life. Then repeat the same process after turning the stone over; if it's big enough, do this again on the other two sides.

Once your conversation with the stone is complete, give reverent thanks as if addressing an old wise man. If it's a hot, dry day and you have a bottle of water, splash some on the stone, as if quenching its thirst before putting it back where you found it.

The more often you do this, the more you'll be able to see Spirit active in the natural world. All of Life is Light; inherent in all of Life is a miracle.

The Oracle of the Speaking Stones

There's another way you can use stones as an interactive oracle tool. You'll need stones no bigger than your thumb that are flat on one side. Find 27 of them, as you'll be using the Universal Unfoldments in Chapter 16. On the flat side of each stone, use dark red, blue, or black nail polish; a dark blue permanent-ink marker; or dark blue paint to write the name or a symbol you create to represent each of the 27 Universal Unfoldments. If you can't find any natural rocks that have the right shape, you can go to an art-supply store and get mosaic tiles, stained-glass tiles, or small wooden blocks. All of these will work.

Make (or buy) a silk, cotton, or leather pouch that's big enough to hold the stones and for you to put your whole hand in to mix them up. To begin, ask for Divine guidance and to be shown the will of Spirit for the highest good of all concerned. Choose one stone for a general overview or course of action; then select three for a reading of past influences, the present, and a possible outcome. Or pick five stones for a reading of past influences, present circumstances, obstacle, right action, and possible outcome.

Always remember to pray for guidance and to accept the answers as they're revealed, and don't repeat the reading. It may take a while to fully understand the meaning implied by the symbols, so spend time meditating on the answer. Keep a journal and pay attention to what you've learned in hindsight.

Also pay attention to the shadow aspects of the symbols if they appear reversed. The reversed symbols point to the difficulties, ego flaws, and challenges that need to be overcome in order for the oracle to be fulfilled.

CHAPTER 16

THE 27 UNIVERSAL UNFOLDMENTS

These Universal Unfoldments are the essential movement of 27 archetypes and influences of the human experience that unfold from birth to death. The images are universal. These are the truths of the world, collected by Spirit since humankind first experienced life and held as markers for us all in our personal and collective evolution.

All of Life follows a common road: We begin our journey as innocents, experiencing our destinies, our fates, and the consequences and influences of our free will—ending the incarnate human journey with wisdom. At different stages, certain universal energies and archetypes will be our prime influences; once we become conscious of them, they can empower us. When brought to awareness, Light is with us. You'll see yourself reflected and your path illuminated in a much deeper and profound way. These aspects will serve to help you understand how energies influence you and how you can work with them to improve your life.

The Protected Child

Oracle meaning: We all begin our journeys as spiritual beings in innocence, and we learn and evolve through our experiences from birth until death. Now is the time for new beginnings and to trust that miracles can and do happen. You'll survive the journey until all your lessons are learned. Right now you're at the beginning, and you may be assured that it's the time to discover what can be learned through risk.

The positive aspects: Innocence, the capacity to survive against all odds, impunity against punishment, optimism, new beginnings, unstable energy without falling

The shadow aspects: Being impetuous, foolish gambling, daydreaming without commitment

Affirmation: With Spirit I am always protected and Divinely directed. I walk toward the Light, and I trust in the love of God [or Goddess, Christ Consciousness, or whatever term you choose].

Planetary influence: Uranus

Number influence: 0

The Shaman

Oracle meaning: You've taken risks and learned many things. You can trust your intellect, for you've earned the first stage of wisdom; your thinking is clear, and your will is strong. You also know that you have everything necessary to make magic, and your work will be rewarded. Anything you begin now will reflect your efforts. Pay attention to all aspects of your life pertaining to communication, and be clear about your words—they can heal as well as cause pain. Be certain of your intention, for your actions will be successful.

The positive aspects: The ability to travel between the perception of the mundane, material world and Spirit; the ability to manifest what's been initiated; empowered communication; the power to turn ideas into reality; the healing arts, medicine, magic, and mystical vision in balance with the intellect

The shadow aspects: The inability to make decisions, failure to complete what is begun, self-deception

Affirmation: The Light within me creates miracles in my life for the highest good of all. It is easy for me to finish what I have begun. I trust in the inspiration of the Divine.

Planetary influence: Mercury

Number influence: 1

The Priestess

Oracle meaning: The Priestess represents the sixth sense and the call to explore the realm of Spirit. She's the aspect within you that links to the Unseen world of Spirit and knows how and when to venture over the line between the material and the spiritual. She represents the Divine feminine and the energy and power of the Goddess. Your intuition is on target, so it's important for you to listen without attachment to your inner voice. You'll make the right decision if you trust your intuitive hunches.

The positive aspects: Intuitive insight, capacity for heightened perception, prophecy, ability to discern the hidden and deeper meanings of life experiences, the symbolic mind (effortless reception of messages from Spirit), understanding the eternal ebb and flow of life, and Goddess energy (the three faces of virgin, fertile mother, and wise woman always together)

The shadow aspects: Repressing the feminine and rejecting, fearing, or refuting intuition

Affirmation: The Light within me leads the way through my intuition. Messages from Spirit come to me effortlessly, and my sixth sense leads me to higher ground. The Soul within me guides me there and teaches me to listen.

Planetary influence: Moon

Number influence: 2

The High Mother

Oracle meaning: All creative projects are meant for success. You're in an important period of fertility and abundance. Pregnancy—both figuratively and literally—will come to fruition as now is the time of expansion. You'll be nourished by Life . . . you just need to allow yourself to trust that it's there.

The positive aspects: Fertility, healthy sustained growth, birth, nourishment, abundance, wealth, love, affection, sensuality, pregnancy, the creative arts, rich harvest, the ability to create with success, clear relationship to your mother

The shadow aspects: Promiscuity, frigidity, inability to express emotions, poverty consciousness

Affirmation: The world is an abundant and rich place with enough for everyone. I co-create my reality with Spirit. I always have enough, and I effortlessly share with others. The Light within me creates miracles!

Planetary influence: Earth

Number influence: 3

The High Father

Oracle meaning: This is the symbol of worldly achievements, and it tells you that your actions can lead to solid foundations for the future. You may receive help from government institutions or banks, or you may find a mentor who can help your progress. This is the sign of upward advancement in any field you choose.

The positive aspects: Strong foundations of personal power, yielding leadership and authority with stability, ensured success, potency, responsibility for others, good governance, the ability for self-discipline

The shadow aspects: Predatory, argumentative, immovable, overly dominant, selfish, power hungry, calculating, lack of ambition, lazy

Affirmation: I am always guided by the Divine to build solid foundations for my life. My goals are met fairly and effortlessly with Spirit as my guide. The Light always shows me the way.

Planetary influence: Mars

Number influence: 4

The Holy Bridge

Oracle meaning: This is the time to ritualize a relationship such as marriage, to legalize partnerships, or to study spiritual matters. It's a sign that you recognize that spirituality is the essence of all of Life. It's the beginning of understanding that religious tradition can be a starting point in creating a personal and direct awareness of the Divine. Pay attention to what you ritualize in your life, and remember that the ritual itself is without meaning on its own; it's only a symbolic bridge used to cross the chasm between material reality and the greater reality of Spirit. Sacred symbols and rites are important, however, because they represent the steps to cross the bridge between worlds. Remember that you're the one who must take those steps in order to reach the Truth.

The positive aspects: Spiritual activity and pursuits, active ritual and symbolism that bridge matter and Spirit, traditional ceremony, marriage, the sanctity of commitment, learning to apply structured wisdom teachings (for example, native shamanism, *A Course in Miracles,* divination systems, meditation, interfaith knowledge, Gnostic mysteries, the study of sacred religious texts, and the like), the ability to see similarities and common themes in faith traditions, spiritual unity

The shadow aspects: Fundamentalism, judgment, being overly secular, religious bias, overreliance on outer appearances

Affirmation: The Spirit within me is the bridge between the finite and the infinite. My soul is immortal and Divinely guided. I release my tight hold on outer appearances and allow the Light within to shine. I follow the signs of the Divine.

Planetary influence: Venus

Number influence: 5

The Lovers

Oracle meaning: This signifies a romantic or general partnership and the opportunity for self-revelation through relationship. It's letting you know that your choices so far have been right to lead you here. This is the time to observe love in your life. How do you tend to it? Perhaps you need to pay more attention to love or make room to allow it to enter. This is a significant time to explore relationships as part of your evolution on your journey to wholeness.

The positive aspects: Romance, love between a couple, eroticism, seeing the body as a temple, the balance of masculine and feminine, threefold union (emotional, physical, and spiritual), the inner marriages of masculine and feminine, personal growth and enlightenment, making healthy choices from a place of balance

The shadow aspects: Triangulation, jealousy, poor boundaries, inability to make choices, manipulation and emotional dishonesty

Affirmation: The Light within me chooses wisely for the highest good of all concerned. I express my love honestly and with integrity. I am always learning from the partners in my life—each soul I connect to shows me a reflection of where I've been, who I am now, and what I need to heal.

Planetary influence: Venus

Number influence: 6

The Liberation

Oracle message: You're in a place where you need to let go and let God lead the way. Trust that opportunities for reward will soon be yours. Sometimes this means an "overnight success," although years of hard work may have preceded it. If you've been constantly turned down and hit brick walls with regard to something you really wanted to achieve, now you have the ability to succeed. You'll find that you have all the energy you need to get things done and the strength of will to do them. If you remember that the Divine is the Higher Power, you won't deplete your own energy. This sign can also pertain to being recognized for your abilities, so use them.

The positive aspects: Victory after hard work, release from "black or white" dual thinking, acting within the laws of Nature, the maturation of the ego/self, a healthy and independent persona, right use of free will, order out of chaos, experiencing the paradox of freedom through surrender

The shadow aspects: Self-will run rampant, arrogance, inability to accept a situation, wrong use of force, addiction, wasting resources

Affirmation: I turn my will and my life over to the care of Spirit. Let the intention of the Divine be done through me. I offer my will and my actions to the highest good of all. I am always in the flow of the natural and highest order of things.

Planetary influence: Mars

Number influence: 7

The Well of Power

Oracle message: This represents your inner strength to overcome any obstacle in your path. No matter what's happening in your life, you'll succeed with patience, generosity, and love as your Source. This may also pertain to your relationship with your companion animal, for unconditional love is an extraordinary well of power. The sign can also relate to someone coming to represent your interests, who will succeed on your behalf.

The positive aspects: Inner fortitude, integrity, generosity of spirit, consciousness beyond the ego; empowerment by faith, courage, and optimism; the promise of success through inner strength rather than outer force; reverence and love for all sentient life

The shadow aspects: Brute force, unconscious action, weakness, lack of courage, fear of failure, fear of the future, mistreatment of animals and nature in general

Affirmation: The Light within me is my source of courage and strength. I see the soul of the world, and I am one within it. It is easy for me to give.

Planetary influence: Sun
Number influence: 8

The Quiet

Oracle message: Take a break and be alone with thoughts of Spirit. Now is the time for nonaction. It's a time to learn about the nature of your question rather than answer it directly. This unfoldment tells you to rest and take a break, to pray and meditate on the true reality, which is the Divine. It may also signify a trip to nature, or to the sea. It's a sign that you must rest to regroup and regain perspective. Immerse yourself in silence for a time to consider all you can to elevate your awareness of your life. You will return with wisdom, and your decision will prove to be prudent and therefore successful.

The positive aspects: Contemplative prayer, meditation, time away, vacation from worldly activities, purification, fasting, awakening the inner world, soul consciousness, gnosis, conscious contact with the Higher Power, direct personal relationship to the Divine

The shadow aspects: Childishness, overreliance on others' opinions, oracle abuse, scapegoating, shallowness, fear of self-evaluation, isolation

Affirmation: I am still so that I may know the will of the Divine. I release my earthly identity and welcome my identity in Spirit. I learn to be in the world, but not of it.

Planetary influence: Pluto
Number influence: 9

Fate

Oracle message: This sign tells you that you're about to encounter aspects of the Divine plan for your life. There are points on the map of potentiality that are preset or preordained before you've come to Earth. Pay close attention to the signs, omens, and synchronicities that unfold in front of you. There are important signals that certain people are meant to come into your life, and circumstances will offer you specific experiences as part of your soul's contract. Jump in, keep your eyes wide open, and be amazed by the extraordinary part you play in the cosmic dance. No matter what happens, everything is a success on the path to awaken to Truth.

The positive aspects: Recognizing Divine synchronicity, fortunate meetings, and opportunities that help shape Destiny; the cycle of birth, death, and rebirth; the four elements of body, thinking mind, intuition, and emotions in balance; expansion, surprises, unexpected good fortune, and opportunities; accepting karma

The shadow aspects: Unexpected delays, struggling against events, accidents, unfortunate timing, seemingly negative experiences that lead to something meaningful and profound, losses that lead to eventual gain

Affirmation: I observe the hand of the Divine in all things; I accept the Mystery and all its surprises. It is easy for me to accept life on its own terms and go with the flow. The Light illuminates my path as I make choices and shape my destiny while fate directs it.

Planetary influences: Jupiter
Number influence: 10

The Truth

Oracle message: No matter what seems unclear at the moment, if you are vigilant, the greater truth will be revealed. Now is the time for rigorous self-appraisal. Have you harmed anyone? Do you need to make amends? Are your affairs in order? It's time to take a look, clean house, and know that within the dance between fate and destiny are steps and missteps—the marks of your choices and the consequences of your actions. Regardless, balance will be restored and the law of karma will play out. Justice will rule in your favor as long as you're honest and forthcoming. If you've suffered, remember that your tears are there to remind you of the Truth that "we all break the same." Until you recognize that you aren't in this world alone, you'll continue to suffer. Whatever happens, freedom is yours as long as you make total acceptance your priority. Seeing things as they really are means that you can expect success—and only then can real change for the better occur.

The positive aspects: Total responsibility for self, self-knowledge, absolute and rigorous honesty, open-minded and active self-appraisal, accepting personal limitations, responding consciously to life, balance between opposing forces, consciousness of personal activity, humility

The shadow aspects: Denial, injustice, imbalance, dishonesty, arguments, lack of humility, over-attachment to material things, refusal to take personal responsibility

Affirmation: I am responsible for my part in the process of my life. I accept responsibility for my past actions so that I may move forward unencumbered by my past mistakes. I have the willingness and the courage to make amends. I love and accept myself.

Planetary influence: Uranus

Number influence: 11

The Sacrifice

Oracle message: Sometimes we have to give up something in order to achieve our hearts' desire. This signifies the cycles of harvest, where a crop has to die in order to generate new life. You may also be required to give up a goal for now, or maybe you need to relinquish security for something that has a more-promising and expansive potential. Success will come if you allow the nature cycle to play out. Still, the paradox of success is dependent on your willingness to be detached from the goal itself. This is what's asked of you right now.

There's another message here as well. In order to see through the eyes of your soul and know the Truth of your spiritual unity with the Divine, the ego's eyes must be closed. In this way, you're being asked to place your material desires on hold and spend this period asking for the Higher Wisdom to be revealed. Waiting will be more than worth the sacrifice.

The positive aspects: Patience, deep inspiration, regeneration through active sacrifice, freely giving up something now so that there will be great things later, peace and understanding through surrender, self-respect, healthy independence, compassion, Christ Consciousness

The shadow aspects: Refusal to accept circumstances, fighting with oneself, pushing against necessary delay, going against the grain, rebellion without purpose, immature selfishness, lack of compassion

Affirmation: I let go and let God. I surrender to what cannot be now, and I release my expectations to the Light. I love and approve of myself.

Planetary influence: Neptune

Number influence: 12

The Phoenix

Oracle message: This is an important time of transformation and hope. Nothing that you set out to do or accomplish will occur the way you thought it would, which is a good thing, because in the death of the old is the birth of something newer and stronger. No matter what, this is the time to let go of old ideas, outmoded relationships that may be draining you, and clutter that may be choking you. Remember that the phoenix is the magical creature that rises up from its own ashes to fly anew with glorious wings. Let go of who you think you are; the Divine within you has bigger plans. If you're suffering some loss, know that within suffering is a jewel of compassion that ignites the bridge between the limitations of mortal vision and the greater Truth of Spirit.

The positive aspects: Letting go of the old to make way for the new, the death of the ego that allows for spiritual transformation, healing through loss, moving from death of the old to rebirth, the eternal triumphs over the transient, transition from mortal to immortal, an important time of inevitable change

The shadow aspects: Holding on to outmoded ideas, fear of change, fear of death, depression, repressed anger

Affirmation: I freely let go of old ideas that no longer serve my highest good. I release my anger and accept the natural cycle of all things. I am a part of Nature and the living manifestation of Spirit. I accept my mortality to celebrate my immortal soul. I am a spark of the Divine and therefore part of a Divine Plan.

Planetary influence: Pluto

Number influence: 13

The Flow

Oracle message: Go with the flow now, and allow your life and the events that present themselves to you to be fluid, as they're meant to be. This isn't the time to control anything, for life is flowing exactly as it's supposed to. Just stay aware and keep conscious contact with the Divine, asking only, "What is the next right action?" You'll receive clear signs and omens to chart your journey, one moment at a time. If you stay to the middle of the river, your boat will always remain intact. All is well in your world. Take no risks at this time; only act when inner calm is the guiding voice.

The positive aspects: Bringing balance through moderation, harmonious action, allowing the blending of opposites to form new life, authentic integrity, the capacity to do the next right action, higher perception as a result of the blending of conscious and unconscious, Spirit and mind, going with the flow of events and responding accordingly with moderate action

The shadow aspects: Trying to control the outcome of events, recklessness, impulsive actions, frenetic activity, obsessive manipulating

Affirmation: It is easy and effortless for me to go with the flow. I am led to inner balance by the Light.

Planetary influence: Venus

Number influence: 14

The Grand Illusion

Oracle message: It's time to take a look at your attachments to the material world. Where do you place your power? Is it in money or a youthful appearance? Are you putting too much attention on the fulfillment of your material desires and pursuing your goals relentlessly? Do you believe that your security lies in the material manifestation of desire? Remember, no matter how much you succeed and get what you want, it will never really fulfill you. You are Spirit evolving through the material world, but in the end you return to Spirit. Don't let your attachments choke the Light out of you. Even the hypnotic pull of a new relationship will not complete you.

That said, you're meant to experience and play in the material realm. Success and failure are all victories in hindsight. Don't be fooled by your own mask or those of others. You have true power within you that's much greater than you can see with your mortal ego eyes. If you look beyond the illusion, you'll be amazed by how great your success can be.

The positive aspects: The release from the illusion of materialism to a greater understanding of Spirit, the life energy of the Kundalini revealed, the implicate power of the Unseen world behind the seen, liberation from desire, the union of spiritual and sexual energy, the practice of Tantra

The shadow aspects: Greed, avarice, obsession with money and status, egocentricity, seeing the material world as the "only reality," lust, gluttony

Affirmation: Spirit is the true reality. The Light shows me the Spirit behind all material things. My desires are natural and pure, and I express them for the highest good.

Planetary influence: Saturn

Number influence: 15

Sacred Lightning

Oracle message: Sudden changes are about to occur and you need to "hang on to your hat." No harm will come to you, even if the world around you seems unstable and disruptive.

The positive aspects: Exhilarating sudden change, positive disruption, revolutionary enlightened change of thought and beliefs, freedom from bondage, unexpected opportunities, sudden mystical revelation, release from the prison of the psyche, clearing of pressure to allow for new growth

The shadow aspects: Imprisonment through self-sabotage, inability to allow growth, being overcontrolling, violence, abusive tendencies, refusal to release repressed material within the psyche

Affirmation: I welcome change. I am always safe and secure. I allow new ideas and beliefs to enlighten me. I am willing to see the world from a higher vantage point.

Planetary influence: Pluto

Number influence: 16

The Great Hope

Oracle message: You are in a place to be hopeful and optimistic because you've overcome a long period of trials and tribulations; look forward with confidence. It's also an appropriate time to help others who are in need, particularly of your hopeful, inspired vision. Any new project can be envisioned now and put into motion. Trust the process of life and you'll be given a glimpse of Truth that will be like a sparkling light in a tunnel, promising the magic of a new life. This is also a sign to tell you to leave space between vision and action. Let things become known to you in their time—no rushing, no pushing. Believe and all will be well.

The positive aspects: Optimism, psychospiritual healing, altruism, inner calm, sensing the unified Spirit in all of Life, conscious connection to the Light, gnosis, the joy of living from a larger worldview and spiritual perception, restored vitality, fresh insights, new horizons to be explored with confidence

The shadow aspects: Insecurity, pessimism, "workaholism," refusing to take breaks, codependency, self-doubt

Affirmation: I see the Spirit in all of Life and I celebrate it with joy. I am always exactly where I need to be. Life inspires me, and I inspire Life. Where there is breath, there is hope.

Planetary influence: Uranus

Number influence: 17

The Dream Time

Oracle message: This is a time to pay attention to your dreams, visions, and psychic experiences. A greater reality is speaking to you unbidden, and messages from Spirit are being sent unsolicited. You need to decipher the messages and go inward and find answers in them. It's also a time to face your fears and nightmares and shed light on them, for fear is only "false evidence that appears real." You're always protected, and you'll always be able to choose goodness over evil. Both are like hungry creatures. Which one will you feed? One will be your greatest ally; the other will destroy you. Always remember that you have nothing to fear but fear itself. Dream and dream well . . . the wisdom of all the living worlds is open to you.

The positive aspects: Experiencing the collective unconscious through dreams, facing primal fears through the passage of imagination, psychic awakening, the power to discern the deepest levels of being, the power of the living myth, bringing wisdom back from non-ordinary reality, conscious access to parallel worlds, angel visitations, connecting to the fairy kingdom

The shadow aspects: Terror of the unknown, manifesting fear into reality, inability to discern fantasy from reality, psychic confusion, lack of symbolic thinking, the dark face of deceit and illusion, obsession

Affirmation: I trust my intuition and listen to my soul's messages. It is easy to navigate the world of dreams, as I always know my way back. There are many faces of reality, all of which are sacred creations of the Divine.

Planetary influence: Moon

Number influence: 18

The Light

Oracle message: The message here is that you have the power to create and manifest your dreams. You'll receive more than you need, and if you make efforts appropriate to your goal, success is certain. What is success? Do you know? Now is the time for you to access a higher Truth about your life and how you'll live it. Everything is Light—that is the Truth. And you're surely on the appropriate path to reclaim your inner Light so that the whole can be restored in Unity. This is also a sign for joy, because you've reached a new level of expression that allows your inner Light to shine on the world for the highest good.

Remember your soul is timeless, never born, and never dies; and when you look at all the life incarnate in the world since the first creation, you'll see endless flickers of light—on, off, on, off. In the brief moment you participate in this endless dance, do you know how you'll shine?

The positive aspects: Illumination, happiness, vital life-force energy, receiving more than what's needed, easily creating abundance and prosperity, effortless manifestation, capacity for lucid thought, purposeful vision, clear and direct understanding of one's purpose—to restore the God-light within to advance the unity of the whole

The shadow aspects: Arrogance, vanity, dreaming without action, delayed success

Affirmation: I am fulfilled beyond measure. It is effortless to manifest with clarity and illumination for the highest good of all. I expect only good, and only good will follow. The Light within me always knows the way and always knows the next right action.

Planetary influence: Sun

Number influence: 19

The Angel

Oracle message: When the Angel appears, you're being asked to follow your inspirations and allow them to manifest without judgment. Everyone has a calling, and it's time to listen to yours. It doesn't have to be a grand gesture. Maybe you're called to help a neighbor, to write songs to inspire others, or to learn to be a healer. Regardless, great or small, the Angel's call will gift you with a Divine touch of grace. It's also time to forgive yourself and others and free yourself from the shackles of negativity. Freedom comes only when you let go and listen for a higher plan. Divine synchronicity is operating in your life, so pay attention and follow the signs. The Angel is whispering your name to do good in the world.

The positive aspects: A deep inner calling for change, the gift of unmerited grace, radical forgiveness, total transformation, evidence of a spiritual awakening, total freedom from addiction and compulsion, good moral judgment, expressing the authentic self, promotion of circumstances, heavenly assistance, rebirth

The shadow aspects: Inability to make decisions, stagnation, compulsive behavior, resentments, envy

Planetary influence: Sun

Number influence: 20

Unity

Oracle message: Now is the time to identify with others instead of comparing yourself to them. When it comes to your goals and aspirations, it's time to look to the bigger picture. How will your actions impact others? See beyond the personal self and look to the whole of the living planet and the collective consciousness. Do your beliefs and attitudes support Life? If not, it's time for a new outlook.

This is also a sign of successful completion, indicating that you have, indeed, gone through a cycle of life and are moving to a higher level of awareness and existence. This is an indication of great strength, humility, authenticity, peace, and compassion for all, as you're able to see through the clear eyes of Spirit as your main source of vision. Celebrate your life as a gift from the Divine. All Life is Sacred, and you're part of the endless flow of energy chosen to express the glory of Spirit.

The positive aspects: Integration of wholeness, knowledge, and wisdom; hearing the Universe as one song and one voice of Life; the unification of Spirit into matter; success; fulfillment; oneness in diversity; the creation of Light; completion of a cycle; the spiral of progress; eternity; immortality; the unity within the Trinity (Father, Son, and Holy Ghost; God, Goddess, and Nature; father, mother, and child; and so on)

The shadow aspects: The illusion of separation, resistance to change, racial prejudice

Planetary influence: Saturn

Number influence: 21

The Great Mystery

Oracle Message: The God Force can never be known or understood by humankind. There is one God behind all faces of the Divine that's ineffable, omniscient, omnipotent, and unknowable. God is the Father, and also Goddess and the Mother. Yet this is only a version of God and not the total Truth. Consciousness and the awareness of spiritual Truth can only be experienced, not taught through dogma and literalism. The Great Mystery can only be known by the soul; it can never be understood by the limitations of the analytical mind. It will always be a mystery until you experience it and behave according to that. Be in the world and not of it, and behave as if the God in all of Life matters.

Only the eternal heart—only Love—knows the way into the Great Mystery and is the answer to it. Be Love today. You're required to walk with faith today and know that the Mystery reveals itself to you in its own terms and not because you demand it.

All aspects are unified; there is no separation into positive and negative.

Affirmation: All is one. All is love. All is well.

Planetary influence: All of them—the Universe; the multi-verse; ordinary, non-ordinary, local, and nonlocal reality; space; time; all that is known or unknown

Number influence: 22

Gaia's Garden

Oracle message: You are of the earth, made of her essence, as is everything that exists here on this planet. In this way you are Gaia's child, offspring of the Great Mother who provides Divine substance to be filled with Spirit. When you understand your relationship to this unfoldment, you'll know your responsibility to every living thing on Earth. Being here and experiencing the manifestation of the material world is a privilege. Remember, you're one with all of the natural world and share it with many other lifeforms. Knowing and committing to do your part to sustain life, acknowledging the Spirit within all of Life—not just humans—as being equal ensures abundance and the continuation of the Garden. Your loving-kindness for Gaia and all her children are called for. In this way, success in all your endeavors is assured.

The positive aspects: Reverence for nature, sustainable community, compassion, empathy, living "green," eco-spirituality, conscious eating, breathing with love and gratitude

The shadow aspects: Littering, waste, animal abuse, overconsumption of water, unconscious living such as the use of pesticides and excessive depletion of natural resources

Affirmation: I am grateful for my life, and I do my part to conserve and heal the planet. I am thankful for the food I eat; I bless the plants and animals who have offered their precious lives so that I may thrive. I treat all living things with respect and kindness. I take only what I need, and I always give back.

Planetary influence: Earth

Number influence: 23

Oceania

Oracle message: Water is the most precious substance. It has the power to be transformed from one state to another and back again without harm. It can move around the greatest obstacles with ease, and it can create a barrier powerful enough to sink a huge ship. It sustains all of Life and is the predominant substance within you. Water rules the emotions and is a powerful symbol of the deepest feelings. At its most profound, Water is the symbol of faith in the Divine.

This is a sign to be fluid, go with the flow, and trust that all things will pass from one state to another. Pay attention to your feelings, experience them, and then allow them to pass away like rivers flowing to the sea. Have faith, and you'll be exactly where you need to be.

The positive aspects: Welcome capacity for change, nonresistance, being in the moment, healthy emotional expression, the art of allowing

The shadow aspects: Rigidity, frigidity, resentments, living in the past or future, obstinate behavior, inability to let go, lack of faith

Affirmation: I always go with the flow. It is easy for me to feel my emotions and let them go. I have the power to transform my life. All is well as I accept fully the current of Divine will through all aspects of my life.

Planetary influence: Neptune
Number influence: 24

The Artist

Oracle message: Spirit is the true essence behind every moment of your experience; everything you accomplish is the result of co-creating with the Divine. The true signs of being in alignment with the Artist—or the creative God Force within you—are passion, love, and authenticity. Each moment that you're on this Earth, you're being invited to awaken to the Truth that within you lies an extraordinary, life-affirming power to create a beautiful, prosperous existence.

Are you engaging in activities you're passionate about? It's time to do so, but you must be careful not to be fixated on the results. It's only when you do what you love for the sake of itself, asking for nothing in return, that Spirit is exalted. It's also important to be fully present and aware that every activity is a co-creation with Spirit, even chopping vegetables or cleaning your house. Make everything you do a sacred act, and your purpose as a co-creator with the Divine will be made crystal clear. If there are blocks, perhaps this is a sign that you're not using all your gifts or that you lack gratitude for what you do have.

This unfoldment is a sign for success in all creative projects that serve the highest good.

The positive aspects: Artistry for its own sake, creative consciousness, total acceptance, surrender to the truth of your present circumstance, vibrant attention, loving what is, fearlessness, authenticity

The shadow aspects: Ego attachment to fame, need for approval, unconscious acts, lack of focus, boredom, refusal to accept circumstances as they are, entitlement, artifice

Affirmation: I am grateful for all I do. Everything in my life is a reflection of my partnership with the Divine. I am excited to co-create with Spirit today. I am a channel for the creative power of Spirit, so I let it guide me to my greatest good. I welcome the higher guidance.

Planetary influence: Mercury

Number influence: 25

Father Time

Oracle message: Time is the temporary illusion of the experience of life on Earth. You're disempowered when too much of your energy is spent ruminating on the past or fixating on a point of arrival in the future. Neither is the Truth of who you really are—these are only stories that have been told and have yet to be told. True destiny, power, and purpose are experienced only when you're fully present in the now. Spirit asks you to be mindful of this moment and to live now no matter what your goals, potentials, or past mistakes. Leave the past behind and disregard the future, for all success is achieved in the here-and-now. No other time matters, for everything is eternal and timeless.

The positive aspects: Living in the present moment, patience, ability to focus on current experiences, mindfulness, being at peace, consciousness of timelessness, past-life memories

The shadow aspects: Fixating on the past or future at the expense of the present moment, continuing patterns of victim consciousness, obsession about aging, fantasy of future opportunities without sustained action, obsessive need to know the future (oracle abuse)

Affirmation: The future is always created in the now. True power lies in the infinite present. I release the past and the future, and I am at peace. I am fully present. I am free in the now, and I am one with the All That Is in this moment, which is eternity.

Planetary influence: All possible aspects of the multi-verse, parallel universes, multi-dimensions

Number influence: 26

CHAPTER 17

THE GUIDE TO SACRED SIGN-BEARERS

This guide will give you a brief outline of animate/conscious and non-animate sacred sign-bearers. While the traditional meanings are provided here, you may have your own karmic or memory experience that will provide alternate personal meanings to the signs. For example, a crab may represent the ability to sidestep an issue or the protection of the hard shell. But if you were born under the astrological sign of Cancer, a crab may indicate your birth month, an event close to your birthday, or the qualities of a Cancerian. The point is that you're invited to understand your own language, which lives within the awareness and consciousness of the collective.

The implications of this guide are universal; all voices are heard and understood as many parts of one song. That's what the Universe is—one song, one Light, one consciousness, all within one Spirit. All of these sacred sign-bearers are part of the one common language of Spirit. Whether you physically encounter them in a synchronistic experience such as actually meeting a wolf in the forest, the essence of wolf visits you in meditation to bring you its awareness, or you see the symbols in a cloud or a cup, their messages share the same soul in the greater essence of Spirit.

Everything is awareness, including you. Because you observe the world, it can exist and interact with you. Your consciousness is your soul, which is in Spirit just as the awareness of the sacred sign-bearers is. Even those beings we consider inanimate, like rocks, have life-force energy. In this way all signs, omens, oracle messengers, messages, and divinations are part of the living language of universal consciousness—which is Spirit, the breath of the God behind all gods, giving life to infinite possibilities. All are mirrors.

I encourage you to explore the guide in detail and refer to the Bibliography for further reading. I've purposely given each sacred sign-bearer the minimum number of words. This allows the descriptions to be like keys to the doors within your own awareness, letting you find the depth of meaning to your personal experience as well as the universal.

On the Ground

Ant: patience, teamwork, industriousness
Antelope: action, energy, grace, swiftness
Armadillo: boundaries, protection, armor, defense against invasion
Badger: digging deep, indirect communication, difficult to injure
Bear: meditating, awakening inner power
Beaver: completing, building, or finishing projects; acting on dreams; manifesting
Beetle: good fortune, renewal, resurrection
Bobcat: listening with intent, discretion, secrets, keeping secrets
Buffalo: answered prayers, gratitude, abundance
Bull: stubbornness, rigidity, gaining through sacrifice
Cat: independence, grace, agility, another chance
Cockroach: indestructible, succeeding against all odds
Cougar: responsible leadership, king of the mountain
Cow: nourishment, getting needs met, maternal love
Coyote: trickster, laughter, pranks, good humor in friendships, hidden lessons

Cricket: invitation to speak, making a phone call
Deer: diplomacy, gentleness, soft bearing, kindness
Dog: loyalty, decency, unconditional love
Earthworm: enjoying the lessons after the storm, opportunities in adversity
Elephant: memory, good fortune, strength and power in community, royalty
Elk: stamina, strength, calm nobility, self-respect
Fox: camouflage, charm, wit, flirtatiousness, being invisible/ visible
Gerbil: rest, retreat, solitude for regeneration
Giraffe: far vision, tall, high achievement
Goat: ambition, upward mobility, sure-footedness
Groundhog: transformation, death without dying
Horse: power, accepting help from others, delegating authority, foreign travel
Jaguar: integrity and impeccability, clear intentions
Kangaroo: getting to the goal, progress assured
Koala: sensitivity, need for isolation
Leopard: swift justice, clarity of vision
Lion: pride, proud accomplishments, generosity
Lizard: detachment, dreamer, creative vision
Lynx: see *Bobcat*
Monkey: ingenuity, curiosity, versatility
Moose: long life, mediumship, cycle of life and death
Mouse: scrutiny, attention to detail, focus
Opossum: pretending, appearances, masks and façades, seeing through them
Panther: letting go of fear, embracing the unknown, welcoming uncertainty
Pig: confrontation, arguments resolved through intelligence
Porcupine: innocence, wonderment, self-protection while exploring new things
Rabbit: fear, running away, needing to trust, not trusting
Raccoon: resourcefulness, theft, thievery, disguises
Ram: ego centered, self-awareness, successful initiation of new beginnings, masculine effort

Rat: intelligence, success, shrewdness, calculation
Rhinoceros: ancient tradition and wisdom, seeking answers in the past
Skunk: self-respect, self-esteem
Snake: healing, letting go of the past, renewal
Spider: creativity, writing, sewing
Squirrel: preparing, saving, storing, resourceful
Tiger: energy, passion, solitary devotion, independence
Walrus: tangible things, money
Weasel: slyness, stealth, calculated movement, behind the scenes
Wolf: teacher, good social order, team leader, fair decisions
Zebra: black-and-white thinking, duality, the blending of opposites

In the Air

Bat: transformation, death and rebirth, facing fear, time of transition
Bee: luck, industry, sweet victory, hard work paying off
Blackbird: positive omen, lack of inhibition, love, spiritual awareness over ego
Blue jay: imitation, taking from others, dishonesty, learning true use of power
Butterfly: beauty, fragility, joy, transmutation
Canary: singing, music, gossip
Cardinal: self-importance, patriarchal power, connection to Christianity
Chicken: sacrifice, abundance through fertility, inner potential
Crane: longevity, keeping quiet about new ideas, self-protection
Crow: higher law, creation, hidden power of the unseen
Dove: peace, prophecy, mourning
Dragonfly: connection to the realm of fairies, seeing through illusions
Duck: comfort, emotional support, connection to family and friends

Eagle: Great Spirit, higher mind, the *I Am,* overview, Big Picture vision

Flea: parasite, taking without giving back, opportunism

Fly: lower ideas, unworthiness, resentments to be healed, clearing emotional garbage

Goose: fidelity, commitment, marriage, positive and successful partnerships

Grouse: higher awareness, acting on connection to Source, personal enlightenment

Gull: the capacity to harmonize potential reality with material success, clarity

Hawk: messenger, letter, phone calls, answers received or on their way, guardianship

Heron: self-reliance, independent thought, survival

Hummingbird: accomplishing the impossible, sweetness of joy, fun

Ladybug: happy-go-lucky, good luck, release of worries

Loon: hopes and dreams rekindled, rejecting compromise, dreams come true

Magpie: opportunities for advancement, impetuousness, scruples, revelation of hidden power

Ostrich: staying grounded, unwavering courage, quiet and steady resolve, avoidance (if head is in the sand)

Owl: deception, self-denial, wisdom from intuition, seeing in the dark

Parrot: individuality, creative self-expression

Quail: abundance in community, family, devotion, group harmony

Raven: magic of synchronicity, ceremonial ritual, healing from illness

Robin: new growth, positive opportunities, safe progress, Christ Consciousness

Stork: babies, new life, successful birth

Swan: clairvoyance, psychic gifts, true inner beauty, transformation

Turkey: sharing, cause and effect, the flow of energy to ensure prosperity

Vulture: misfortune, gloating, jealousy, insensitivity

Wasp: anger, retaliation, warning to protect oneself

From Water

Alligator: flexibility, nonjudgment, thoughtful integrative action
Chameleon: adaptability
Crab: indirect action, hidden sensitivity, avoiding issues
Dolphin: playfulness, flirtation, spontaneity, telepathic communication
Fish: abundance and prosperity assured, dualism
Frog: cleansing, cleaning house (literally and figuratively)
Octopus: possessiveness, dexterity, ability to multitask
Otter: playfulness, affection, loving nature, femininity
Penguin: endurance in spite of conditions, lucid dreaming
Seal: imagination, focus on manifesting dreams, clarity of purpose
Sea lion: masculine strength, swimming through turbulent times
Sponge: education, learning, absorbing new ideas
Turtle: slow and steady, connection to Gaia (Mother Earth) energy
Whale: connection to ancestral memory, collective unconscious

Trees

Acacia: knowing how to let something die for something new to take its place, mystical death and rebirth of the psyche
Alder: prophetic insight, blending strength and courage with compassion and generosity
Apple: joyful sharing, positive sign for healing, the law of attraction, you reap what you sow
Ash: strength and wisdom, awareness of connectivity, belonging, filling the God-shaped hole within
Aspen: facing inner doubt, love overcomes fear
Bamboo: luck, prosperity, balance
Beech: writing, the form of language, carrying a message, tolerance, prayer
Birch: clearing out old ideas, purification and strong renewal, new dimensions of awareness, a fresh start

Blackthorn: time to face the shadow self, causing pain to others, self-sabotage

Broom: clean up your act, declutter, radical self-care

Cactus: strength and endurance in any condition

Cedar: protection and cleansing

Cherry: new awakenings and insight

Cypress: understanding karma, wisdom from adversity

Elder: death, rigorous self-appraisal

Elm: reliance on intuition

Eucalyptus: clear connection to Spirit, clarity of thought/dreams

Fig: prosperity built on understanding the past

Gorse: great optimism, faith, the sun, hope emerging from disappointment

Hawthorn: fertility, creativity, lovemaking, connection to fairies

Hazel: inspiration from meditation, distilling knowledge into wisdom, communication, teaching and learning

Heather: sacrifice; accountability for all actions; balance between self-expression, free will, discernment

Hickory: persistence

Holly: clarity of purpose, personal sacrifice, calmness, diplomacy

Honeysuckle: endurance, adaptability

Ivy: cycle of life and death, the search for enlightenment, warning against getting caught in a situation resulting in loss of power

Joshua tree: uniqueness, wisdom, strength in maturity

Lemon: love and friendship, cleansing of old wounds

Lilac: clairvoyance, balance between intellect and Spirit

Magnolia: test of faith

Mango: sensitivity, need to watch oversensitivity, heightened intuition/telepathy

Maple: male/female balance

Mistletoe: romance, love, feminine sexuality

Oak: endurance, successful manifestation

Olive: peace and harmony

Orange: letting go of fear, healing deep emotional wounds

Palm: protection

Peach: artistic beauty, longevity

Pine: farsightedness and the need for objectivity, awakening the heart, releasing guilt, arousing the inner Divine

Poplar: help coming to manifest dreams

Redwood: timeless wisdom, new perspectives out of ancient vision

Rowan: self-control, developing discernment, wise discrimination

Spruce: calming, the need to soothe and protect

Sycamore: nourishment, beauty, admiration

Walnut: freedom gained by initiating transitions

Willow: surrendering to emotion, releasing sadness, blocked emotions' need for expression, revealing hidden things, awakening the subconscious

Yew: transcendence, resurrection, rebirth, sum of all wisdom

Flowers and Plants

Aloe: time to heal, capacity to heal others

Angelica: angelic communication

Baby's breath: gentleness, modesty

Basil: discipline and devotion

Begonia: commitment to enriching activities

Buttercup: self-worth, empathy, compassion

Carnation: new love, deepening affections

Chrysanthemum: vitality, youthful life force

Corn: new abundance and prosperity assured

Daffodil: inner beauty, self-care

Daisy: spiritualizing the intellect, connection to fairies and nature spirits

Dandelion: looking beyond the surface

Frangipani: need to set higher goals

Gardenia: telepathy

Garlic: psychic protection

Geranium: new happiness

Goldenrod: positive focus, energy to complete projects

Hibiscus: libido, sexual energy
Hyacinth: overcoming jealousy
Iris: birth, peace restored
Jasmine: prophetic dreams
Lily: humility, empathy
Lotus: higher spiritual knowledge
Morning glory: spontaneity
Orchid: seduction, sensuality
Peony: strong artistic abilities
Peppermint: trusting protective energies
Petunia: enthusiasm, energy
Poppy: sleep, time to rest
Rose: love, heart connection
Rosemary: positivism
Sage: communication with Spirit, divination, higher consciousness
Snapdragon: assertiveness, self-reliance, protective action
Sunflower: happiness, gaiety, dancing
Tiger lily: overcoming base emotions
Tobacco: prayers answered
Tulip: trusting own efforts
Violet: luck, good fortune
Water lily: tangible wealth and money
Zinnia: courage pays off

Magical Creatures

Angel: protection, guidance, sign from Spirit
Cupid: romance, love, partnership
Dragon: strength of will, power, protection, opposition
Dwarf: solid foundations, slow movement
Elf: fun, lightheartedness
Fairy: inspired ideas, spending time in nature
Goblin: wounded ego, negativity
Phoenix: rebirth and strength after great loss
Unicorn: innocence, acting on pure faith in the Unseen

Common Objects and Recognizable Symbols

These are self-explanatory as well as divinatory in meaning. They should be seen as Spirit participating in the stories as they reflect the circumstances—symbolic or literal—of your life. As you begin to understand the metaphoric language of Spirit, your awareness will expand and reveal a much deeper aspect of life than you're used to seeing in the material. Remember, the entire world is ensouled. There's a greater spirit implicated even in human-made objects.

This is a short list of examples of possible shapes, images, real objects, and events that may reveal themselves within an oracle message, omen, or sign. I've included the minimum of universal and specific interpretations to trigger your own experience of how they could apply to you. You might like to write your own list of objects that have special meaning to you, in addition to what's here.

Remember that when Spirit uses symbolic language to speak with you, the conversation may take place in all kinds of ways. You might see these signs and symbols through your peripheral vision, out of the corner of your eye, or gazing at a cloud; or your senses could become amplified while you're reading the paper or watching a movie. You may see an image repeatedly over a few days, perhaps while driving the car, sitting in nature, or listening to the radio.

For example, if you see a raven on TV, then notice it intuitively again as the bird perches outside your house, see the name Raven as someone's signature on a piece of paper, and then dream of one at night, you're receiving a sign to pay attention to the magical synchronicities that are aligning in your life to point the way on your highest path!

Here's a beginning for you to explore the language of Spirit. Keep a sign journal and add your own symbols as you open up the conversation. You'll be amazed by how chatty Spirit really is.

A

Ace: got an ace up your sleeve and you may not even know it, a sign of talent and ensured success

Acorn: new idea with sacred potential for long-term transformation and power

Airplane: travel by air, freedom, great inspired ideas revealed

Altar: self-sacrifice, a place of worship and ritual

Amethyst: guards against intoxication, protects the third eye, sign of psychic development

Anchor: staying home, feeling of security in one's surroundings, someone else's agenda to keep you in one place

Apple: sacred fruit of Avalon, totality of wisdom, totality in general, represents earthly desires

Ark: preservation and protection of the material and spiritual, safe journey through turbulent times, ensured rebirth

Arrow: getting to the point, meeting objectives, the way is correct and clear, travel by air

Ax: inner capacity to cut through illusion and get to the truth; potential or fear of loss; enforced loss that leads to something much better; clearing the way for new growth; letting go of old ideas, people, places, and things that no longer serve the highest good; potential of divorce

B

Baby: new and wonderful things untainted and innocent, pregnancy, a sign to nurture and tend a new project or idea, being a novice at something

Baggage: unresolved emotional issues from the past, carrying the burdens of others, a sign to clear the baggage that prevents you from moving forward

Ball: a game and it's your turn to take action

Balloon: floating away or popping represents powerlessness and shattered illusions, floating in the sky is all about joy and happiness

Bandages: healing time, nursing wounds

Basket: pay attention to what you're carrying

Bathtub: time to clean up loose ends, cleanse yourself of a situation

Bed: active subconscious, need to rest, potential illness, pay attention to self-care, pay particular attention to the content of dreams

Bell: all creative energy is suspended between Spirit and matter, music and creativity, a call to manifest your dreams with joy

Blue: color of throat chakra, communication of all sorts (need to speak to someone about something)

Boat: being taken to safety; exploring new things without fear; leaving a situation and sailing away; if sinking, jump ship and swim to safety

Bomb: explosive situations that need particular self-protection now, being aware of explosive reactions as something may be destroyed in the process

Book: time for study, life lessons

Boots/shoes: someone walking all over you, time to walk away from something

Bottle: examining what's contained in your life (joy or confusion), emptying out what you don't want, needing to "take your medicine," alcoholism

Boulder: something too large to move by your own efforts (needs a team), a block in plans or inner self, walk around something and don't try to attack it head-on

Box: something needs to be put away or contained, a safe place, being boxed in

Bridge: desire to change, a symbol of safe transition

Brush (hair): brushing away difficulties, time to smooth things over, taking action to alleviate unresolved issues, time to clean house

Building: represents the architecture of your life, is what you're doing at present built on solid foundations?

C

Candle: illumination, creative inspiration, optimistic outcome, Light of the Divine

Cape: disguised motives, check own motives, a miracle is coming (if it looks like Superman's cape)

Car: desire for travel, upcoming move, movement in general

Castle: very well-protected treasure, reaching a goal and being a leader (king/queen of the castle)

Caution sign: need to be cautious

Cave: solitude and the need to rest and meditate, things that are hidden and not yet ready to be revealed

Cemetery: Death, leaving things behind that are no longer needed, circumstances that have died, endings

Chair: time for a break, time to get to work in the chair, meditation

Church (or temples, mosques, and the like): honor Spirit, pray, meditate, prayers have been heard, Spirit resides within all things in the material world

Cliff: being at the edge of something, pay attention to your steps (be cautious), a major change

Clock: time ticking, pay attention to time, favorable timing, time is of the essence

Closet: hiding something, shyness, a call to come out and play

Clown: be joyous, take pleasure in life, have more fun

Cobwebs: having too many ideas at once, being too focused on the past, a time to avoid intrigue, a foggy mind

Cocoon: period of waiting before something is ready, a safe place of refuge

Comet: a sign of absolute victory, Divine interference

Crown: a sign of assured success and authority

Crystal: pay attention to all facets of a situation, something will be amplified, Spirit

Cup: vessel of Spirit, the way you're perceiving things at the moment, emotions, a marriage

D

Desert: a time of emptiness, nonaction, no end in sight, patience required

Door: moving from one experience or state to another, the marker between the material and the spiritual

Doormat: letting someone walk all over you

Drum: natural rhythm of life, issues pertaining to the heart, a shamanic vehicle to travel into the spiritual world

Dunce cap: stupidity, education, time to study something

Dungeon: punishment, feeling trapped, warning of a relationship that may be too controlling, being taken "hostage"

E

Ear: need to listen more, pay attention to what you hear

Earth: the material world, Gaia, stability, grounded ideas

Egg: birth, pure potential, prosperity

Elevator: transportation between states of consciousness, going up or down in a situation

Emerald: love and compassion, matters of the heart

Excrement: need to release something, someone lying, detoxify life in general

F

Feather: angelic realm, connector between the immortal Spirit world and mortal world, Spirit is protecting you

Fire: creativity, optimism, sexual energy, anger, a temperamental "fiery" personality

Flood: emotional overwhelm, a situation that's out of control

Flowers: happiness, celebration, connection to the realm of the fairies

Fog: inability to see clearly, a temporary need to rest (pay close attention to what you see after the fog)

Food: nourishment, abundance

Forest: nature, a refuge, growth and fertility, a need for direction indicates waiting for another sign

Fountain: a wellspring of happiness, abundance, joy, youthful qualities, great spiritual energy, emotional cleansing, laughter

G

Garbage: something needs to be thrown out in your life, something has lost its service or usefulness, lack of integrity

Garden: bounty possible in the material world, fruitful manifesting that must be tended to, remember to weed your "garden of negativity"

Glasses: pay attention to detail

Glove: diplomacy, etiquette, social boundaries, an impending fight (boxing glove)

Gold metal: money, tangible evidence of manifesting your dreams, spiritual goodness

Grandfather: wise man, ancestral wisdom

Grandmother: wise woman, crone, feminine goddess, wisdom

Grave: transformation through endings, someone's passing

Green: love, healing, personal growth, Light

Guitar: creativity, music, seduction, the bardic tradition of storytelling and mythmaking, the music playing in your life

Gun: self-protection, male sexuality, aggression

H

Hair: natural adornment, attention to self-image, freedom of expression (as in hair blowing in the wind)

Hammer: mystical power of manifestation, power to build or destroy a situation

Hands: protection, authority, donation, prayers answered, the outer physical projection of the inner world

Happy face: joy, contentment, need to be happy and focus on the good rather than the negative

Harp: the accompaniment of angels, a bridge between heaven and the mortal world

Heart: love, the center of the illuminated spiritual expression of unity

Hole: gateway from one dimension to the other, pure potential, unknowable Mystery of life, flaw or wound in the fabric of reality

Home: consciousness, the inner mind, safe place

Hood: invisibility, sacred purpose, commitment to a higher view

Horn: plenty and abundance, warning to protect yourself from outside influences or from inner destructive ones

House: see *Home*

I

Ice: frozen emotions (element of water) or something frozen in the past, instability and a warning that the direction you're taking is dangerous ("thin ice")

Iceberg: only seeing a small part of what's really going on, go deeper to find the real truth and substance

Icicle: melting emotions, positive emotional change

Indian (Americas): Spirit in nature, achieving balance by learning about the old ways of the indigenous peoples

Indicator light: check your direction

Indigo: color of transcendent spirituality, raise your vibration and meditate, contemplate Spirit

Interior (of a place): the inner world of the mind, pay attention to your thoughts and how they're placed

J

Jack-o'-lantern: sign of autumn, connecting to the immortal consciousness of a loved one who has passed over

Jail: restriction, being in a prison of your own making

Jewel: treasure, things of value, spiritual and material wealth

K

Key: opening the door to a new perception, pointing to right action

King: authority, government, taxman, husband

Kite: higher self, listening to intuition

Knife: cutting words, need to be mindful of deception and betrayal

Knot: marriage, partnership, unhealthy enmeshment, disentangle from a situation

L

Ladder: movement out of difficulty into a more positive situation, seeking higher goals, promotion

Lake: dreams, emotions, consciousness, reflection of emotional states, ability to see into the future

Letter: direct communication, message

Lighthouse: illumination of your path, ideas coming of how to reach an objective

Lightning: big ideas, unexpected change, sudden loss leading to better things, being powerless over others

Logs: shelter, building upon natural talents and skills, authenticity, purpose

M

Magician: illusion, deception, trickster, need for more real magic in your life, spiritual perception
Mermaid: emotional rescue, finding magic by going to the ocean
Mirror: all Life is a reflection
Money: materialism, manifestation, wealth
Moon: psychic intuition, prescient dreams, Goddess energy
Mountain: prayer, journey to the Higher Self, large obstacle to overcome, ensured success after long and arduous work
Musical instrument: harmony, taking steps to restore harmony

N

Nails: anxiety, hard work, putting the finishing touches on something to make it secure
Nakedness: being exposed, integrity, truthfulness, being without artifice
Numbers: see Chapter 13
Nuts: reminder to save, assurance of security

O

Obelisk: illumination, the rays of the sun shining into the material manifestation of the world
Ocean: collective consciousness, emotions, deep contemplative thought, endless potential and possibility
Office: sign of order, organization, professional work
Officer: authority, need to police something, resolving guilt
Onion: peeling the layers of self to get to Spirit, situation that may bring tears
Orange: intimacy, relationships, sexuality, creativity, procreation
Orchestra: symbolic of cohesive teamwork, a corporation
Orgy: chaos, gluttony
Oyster: hidden value

P

Pearl: natural hidden talents newly revealed, a gift, pleasant feelings

Pedestal: warning not to elevate the material above the spiritual

Pendulum: choices not yet taken, hidden meanings

Pen or pencil: time to journal or write, legacy, signing legal documents

Piano: music, self-expression, harmony between opposites

Pills: healing

Pink: unconditional love

Pond: restful emotions, emotional healing

Purple: psychic phenomena, the third eye, clairvoyance, prescient dreams, prophecy, royalty

Q

Quartz: events will be amplified, clear Spirit connection

Queen: feminine authority, friendships among women, Goddess energy, positive result from following intuition

Quicksand: impossible circumstances, unforeseen dangers ahead, a sense of overwhelm, need to be careful of actions and the current direction

Quill: difficult consequences from foolish action, need to avoid impulsive behavior

R

Radar: awareness, hypervigilance, clairsentience, reading between the lines

Radio: clairaudience, intuition, reminder to pay attention to what you hear from others, Cledons, spontaneous oracles

Rain: disappointment, sadness, unexpected delays, new growth after rainy times, need to resolve repressed grief

Rainbow: promised relief after stormy experiences

Red: family issues, money, real estate, security, inheritance, physical health

Ring: marriage, engagement, eternity, commitment

River: the continuation of life, forever changing, forever moving

Road: the journey itself, staying true to your path, the true unfoldment of destiny, fate and free will

Robber: being stolen from, reminder to pay attention to the way you spend your time, "stealing" from someone else, warning to be impeccable

Rock: something stable and old, traditional, looking to the past for knowledge

Rope: a way out, restraints, help is coming

S

Saddle: being held firmly in place as you travel through life, time to move, feeling burdened by others or by too many projects and obligations

Salt: true integrity, authenticity, preservation, purification

Sand: the passing of time, insignificance, humility, being one among many, small irritations that will pass

Saw: getting to the core of something, concepts that will build upon others, cutting-edge ideas

Scissors: cutting away the extraneous things of life, creative projects such as sewing

Shadow: the darker aspects of the psyche, unresolved emotional wounds that show up in behavior

Shoes: time to take action

Shovel: digging deep for the truth, addressing the psyche (possibly through therapy)

Statue: lifelessness, a likeness but not the true essence, image

Steps: a series of actions taken and that are still to be taken

Stop sign: warning not to proceed with the current direction

Storm: conflict between friends, inner conflict that's causing anxiety

Sun: all your needs will be met, spiritual illumination, happiness, joy

Swamp: being bogged down, tired, unclear, take action by doing something against your routine

Sword: defensiveness, need to defend yourself, the power to wound, sharp intellect, power to fend off negativity

T

Table: clear speech, laying your "cards on the table"

Tap: control emotions, pay attention to leaks of information, gossip

Tape: measure and compare your intentions to your actions, time to take inventory of your thoughts and deeds, make amends if you need to

Tapestry: the patterns of life, pay particular attention to the stories you tell about yourself

Target: stay out of the way of others' anger, reaching a goal on time

Tattoo: making your mark

Tea: gentle refinement, qualities of elegance, stimulating discussions

Teacher: energy of life's lessons

Teeth: ancestral traits, issues pertaining to inherited circumstances

Telegram: important messages (possibly life-altering)

Telephone: time to reach out to others, an invitation to community

Temple: a sacred place

Tent: a temporary place, transitions that lead to temporary instability

Thorn: the pleasure and pain of love, natural protection from offense

Thread: element of joining together through concepts or experiences

Throne: seat of authority, requirement to be fair and just

Thumb: direction of success (up or down), inner approval or dis-approval, a measure of self-worth and self-esteem

Thunderbolt: revolution, rebellion with just cause, great ideas

Tightrope: warning to tread carefully, great skill and balance required to continue the path you're on

Tires: continual small changes, possible road trip ahead

Toilet: flush unnecessary and superfluous situations, need to let go of something

Tombstone: looking at the past; end of a cycle; warning that a circumstance, project, or relationship is coming to an end; death of affection; passing over

Toys: time to play more, playing without meaning, lack of sincerity

Train: heading in the correct direction, travel by train

Train tracks: strategize, set goals, and make plans

Treasure: gifts of value, tangible evidence of dreams coming true, windfalls, wealth of experience and knowledge, education

Trees: the Life of all things, from spark to seed to sapling to tree; consistent; regenerative; ancient; the representative of Spirit giving life to matter; never-ending life

Trident: three-pronged instrument of the god Poseidon/Neptune, piercing emotions, the power of the trinity of mind/body/spirit, piercing through illusion

Trumpet: important news coming, importance of being heard

Tunic: the mask of profession, role-playing

Tunnel: a passage into temporary darkness, situation requiring faith and trust in a higher purpose

U

UFO: something alien and unknown, a feeling of being intruded upon, fascination with the unknown, new and uncharted experience

Umbrella: protect yourself from overemotionalism, shelter is available, father image, a time of mourning, a funeral

Uncle or aunt: friendly and helpful people

Undertaker or ferryman: complete projects, pay attention to details, take care of loose ends, endings, the potential of new life

Urn: being contained and protected, oneness and the prosperity and abundance inherent therein, protection of the Divine feminine

Utensils: pay attention to how things function, figure out steps that need to be taken in order to complete something or what things go together

V

Valley: peaceful contemplation, rest and recharge, time to enjoy life, place and time for contemplating intentions before manifesting

Vampire: a predatory personality, usury, disengage from any person or situation that drains you

Vase: acceptance, containment of emotions, elegance

Vehicle: depending on size, type, and speed, expresses physical body, mood, current experience of life (a bumpy ride in a big truck can mean things will be temporarily difficult and you may feel like a bull in a china shop, but this too shall pass)

Vines: pay close attention to intuition, deadlines, or decisions creeping up; the flow and insistence of the creative impulse

Violin: victim consciousness, seduction or serenade, sadness

Volcano: volatile personality, disruptive circumstances, upsetting news

Vomit: refusal to accept circumstances, gluttony

Vulva: feminine sexuality, procreation, receptivity, pregnancy

W

Wallet: hidden value, talents not yet expressed, personal currency and life purpose, abundance, prosperity, poverty consciousness (if empty)

War: turmoil, conflict, arguments must be avoided, possible violence

Watch: measure of time, all things occur on the universe's timetable (not necessarily your own)

Water: emotions, consciousness, fluidity, need to be flexible and go with the flow

Wave: ride the wave and go with the flow

Wax: substance that grounds illumination, knowledge that allows for inspiration, malleability, some circumstance can be changed and molded

Web: personal connections and synchronicities, being caught in intrigue, creative writing, music, sewing, crafts

Wheel: constancy of change, eternity, movement and travel, changing cycles of mortality in balance with the constant of immortality

White: Spirit, purity, virginal, untouched, clean

Window: a sign of a new worldview, capacity to observe the direction of a transition from one state of consciousness or concept to another, new ideas

Wine: the good life, abundance, drinking the sacred, communion with Christ Consciousness, drunkenness

Wings: flying by air, angelic protection, difficulties will be overcome

Witch: wise woman, healer, magic, spiritual alignment with natural forces

X

X-ray: the capacity to see through things, reminder to look closely and read between the lines, warning against being too transparent

Y

Yellow: personal power, intelligence, analytical thought
Yield sign: slow down, time for compromise

Z

Zodiac: aspects of the evolution of the psyche, reincarnation, past-life information, themes and archetypal experiences during the span of human life, the cycle from birth to death to rebirth
Zone: an area specific to your inquiry, specialization, specific part of something

Sacred Symbols

Ankh: spiritual wisdom, longevity
Arrow: clear direction
Celtic cross: illumination
Chalice: sacred quality, holiness, spiritual abundance and joy
Christian cross: redemption through sacrifice, necessary death of the ego
Circle: boundless unity
Hch'ai: life-force energy
Hexagon: Divine mind, healing star, absolute balance
Infinity sign: infinite perfection
Om: sound of eternal life; four stages of consciousness: awake, sleeping, dreaming, transcendence
Pentagram: forces of the earth
Red cross: altruism, help
Spiral: path to wholeness, continual change, evolution of the universe
Square: earth
Star: guidance from above, ideas and inspiration revealed, hope
Triangle: trinity, stability

Human Features, Expressions, and Gestures

These are self-explanatory, and you can imagine for yourself their greater meaning in context with other signs and symbols.

- **Eye(s):** open, shut

- **Nose**

- **Mouth:** frowning, smiling, open

- **Lips:** pursed, pouting, tight, puckered

- **Ear(s)**

- **Hands:** in prayer, outstretched, cupped, waving, saluting, in fists

- **Breast**

- **Genitals**

- **Facial expressions:** happy, sad, shocked, bored, rapt

- **Baby, mother, family group, religious figures**

Now you have a brief introductory guide to the sacred sign-bearers who may cross your path to engage you in a dialogue with Spirit. Although there are more than 400 listed here, there are hundreds more. Ancient and indigenous cultures have rich traditions that honor the Spirit in all things. If you want to learn more about this and explore the subject of living sacred symbols in the natural world more extensively, please refer to the Bibliography.

Review these lists and get to know the symbols. Perhaps you've had personal experiences that may add to their meaning. Invite each symbol to reveal more of itself to you—maybe you'll receive a flash of insight. Always remember to keep a written record of your experiences.

This process can't be forced and always reveals itself gently, surely unfolding as you allow it to. Just remember to slow down, breathe deeply, and be open to experience a greater awareness of the world. The wisdom of Spirit is always available. It takes time to process, interpret, and understand the dialogue, too. Mystical revelation comes of its own accord as you go deeper in the dialogue, letting go of your old ideas, prejudices, and limitations. The magic of life will always be revealed if you're patient.

AFTERWORD

My intention for this book is to encourage you to experience a new way of seeing the world and engaging with it from the perspective of being One with Spirit. All of the stories, exercises, and ideas expressed here were included with the commitment of honoring lost but once-venerated traditions of conversing with the world of Spirit for guidance. The world of oracles, omens, and signs is universal, sacred, and accessible to anyone who desires a greater and deeper experience of Life—messages from Spirit are for all of us. I invite you to visit my Website, **www.colettebaronreid. com**, to explore this subject further.

Always remember who you are—Spirit first, human second. You're more than you know, and the world you see is but a tiny part of an Infinite Intelligence that's everywhere in everything.

Remember that when you look into the world, Spirit will always be looking back at you. When you need to be heard, Spirit will be listening. So let there be Light and come and see the world in the truth of Unity. Spirit has many messages for you. Come learn, listen, and know . . . you are loved.

ACKNOWLEDGMENTS

Of course there are too many people to thank and not enough pages in this book. Sincere and heartfelt thanks to my wonderful husband, Marc, who tolerated my many unpredictable moods throughout the birthing process of this baby. I love you more than ice cream, chocolate, and shopping. You are my world—you and our fur babies.

To my wonderful assistant, Michelle, for holding down the fort and being so nice to all the hundreds of people trying to get appointments while I buried myself in my writing. I adore you.

Thank you from the bottom of my heart to Mrs. Kelly. I know you're watching me from Spirit and enjoying every minute of this ride.

Thank you to my hero Reid Tracy and the marvelous Louise Hay. Y'all rock my world.

To my soul sister Nancy Levin: You make touring a poet's dream. To Sylvia Browne: May you always have flowers and beauty surrounding you. To Dr. Wayne Dyer: Your support has meant so much to me, and I'm incredibly grateful. To Mama Maya—I love you so!

To my fantabulous editor Angela Hynes: I'm ever so grateful for your graceful and intelligent approach to actually helping me create a book out of all that mountain of writing, and for tolerating my neuroses with such kindness. I get first dibs on you next year! And to the fantastic and talented editorial and design staff with Hay House—I am so privileged to work with you: Jessica Kelley, Lisa Mitchell, Amy Rose Grigoriou, and Tricia Breidenthal.

For the lovely Jill Kramer: I invoke the Goddess for a vision of leather and the sea.

To Denise Linn: As always, a gazillion thanks for your steady and generous friendship and words of constant wisdom.

To Justine Picardie: For your consistent and wonderful support, I adore you.

To my favorite visionary, Gregg Braden: Thank you so much for your generosity and those hours of phone calls explaining the meaning of the Universe. I think I need to read your next book.

To Timothy Freke and Peter Gandy for all that amazing stuff on Gnosticism.

Special thanks to: Dr. Darren Weissman, Dr. Alvin Pettle, Dr. Noel Solish, and Dr. Nitin Dilawri.

To John Holland for your friendship and wisdom.

To Robert Ohotto for your brilliance and great conversation.

To Donna Abate and Gracie Girl: Your Colette loves you—xoxox.

Thank you so very, very, very much to my dear friend Diane Ray, the lovely Flowdreamer Summer McStravick, Sonny Salinas, Joe, Kyle, and Emily, and anybody else I missed at Hay House Radio.

A special thank-you (in no particular order) to my love children Mollie, Matty, Christa, and Adrian; to Mike Fishell, my favorite bodyguard; everyone at Hay House UK: Michelle, Jo, Nicola, and Louise; and Leon Nacson and the folks at Hay House Australia.

A very special thank you to all the people who allowed me to include their wonderful stories for this book. Your sharing will touch so many—I'm eternally grateful for your contributions. And a very special mention to those whose stories didn't make the book because of space constraints. Your wonderful contributions will appear on the accompanying Website with the greatest of thanks and gratitude.

Acknowledgments

Many thanks to: Adriene Dillon, Althea Grey, Bessie, Beth Richards-Mastin, Brenda Lacasse, Catherine Hahn, Christine Agro, Dale McCarthy, Deborah Samuel, Deb Vitris, Dee Carroll, Deenah Mollin, Dovile Mark, Gail Ingson, Gord Ridell, Heather Dietrich, Janelle Woods, Jelena Nonveiller, Jennifer Evans, Joanne Morgan, Jodi Menke, Juli Gumbiner, Katarina Alexander, Kathy Ryndak, Kellie Monaghan, Kim White, Kimberly Hardie, Lenka Slivova, Linda Horn, Lori McDaniel, Lucy Cavendish, Madge Barnes, Marcy, Mary Aver, Mei Wei Wong, Michelle Hughes, Mischelle Finley, Nathan Harley, Nora Kidd, Renee Anzures, Richard Hastings, Sandy Powell, Sophie Craighead, Tammy Kennedy, Tania Gabrielle, Tekeyla Friday, Terry Bowen, and Wachan Bajiyoperak.

To all my friends (and you know who you are): I send you my deepest thanks for understanding that I need to disappear when I write. Thanks for still being there when I'm done. I love you all.

My deepest gratitude is of course for Spirit and the God behind all Gods and Goddesses, who makes everything real.

Blessed be.

Andrews, Ted. *Animal-Speak: The Spiritual & Magical Powers of Creatures Great & Small.* Llewllyn Publications, 1993

———. *Nature-Speak: Signs, Omens & Messages in Nature.* Dragonhawk Publishing, 2004

Armstrong, Karen. *A History of God: The 4000-Year Quest of Judaism, Christianity and Islam.* Ballantine Books, 1993

Bluestone, Sarvananda. *How to Read Signs and Omens in Everyday Life.* Destiny Books, 2001

Braden, Gregg. *The Isaiah Effect: Decoding the Lost Science of Prayer and Prophecy.* Three Rivers Press, 2000

———. *The God Code: The Secret of Our Past, the Promise of Our Future.* Hay House, 2004

Chernak McElroy, Susan. *Animals as Guides for the Soul.* The Ballantine Publishing Group, 1998

Cirlot, J. E. *A Dictionary of Symbols.* Philosophical Library, Inc., 1971

Cunningham, Scott. *Divination for Beginners: Reading the Past, Present & Future.* Llewellyn Publications, 2003

Drury, Nevill. *Sacred Encounters: Shamanism and Magical Journeys of the Spirit.* Watkins Publishing, 2003

Farmer, Steven D., Ph.D. *Animal Spirit Guides: An Easy-to-Use Handbook for Identifying Your Power Animals and Animal Spirit Helpers.* Hay House, 2006

Fiery, Ann. *The Book of Divination.* Chronicle Books, 1999

Harner, Michael. *The Way of the Shaman.* HarperSanFrancisco, 1990; originally published by Harper & Row, 1980

Joseph, Peter (producer). *Zeitgeist, the Movie.* **www.zeitgeistmovie. com**

Judith, Anodea. *Eastern Body, Western Mind: Psychology and the Chakra System as a Path to the Self.* Celestial Arts Publishing, 1996

Lawrence, Shirley. *Exploring Numerology: Life by the Numbers.* The Career Press, Inc., 2003

Linn, Denise. *The Secret Language of Signs: How to Interpret the Coincidences and Symbols in Your Life.* Ballantine Books, 1996

Lyle, Jane. *Tarot.* The Hamlyn Publishing Group Ltd., 1990

Martin, Ted. *Psychic and Paranormal Phenomena in The Bible: The True Story.* Psychicspace Company, 1997

Pollack, Rachel. *Seventy-Eight Degrees of Wisdom: A Book of Tarot.* Thorsons Publishing Group, 1997; original Dutch edition of *Seventy-Eight Degrees of Wisdom: Part I, The Major Arcana* published by Uitgeverij W. N. Scors, Amsterdam, 1980

Sams, Jamie, and David Carson. *Medicine Cards: The Discovery of Power Through the Ways of Animals.* St. Martin's Press, 1999

Schwartz, Gary E., Ph.D., and William L. Simon. *The G.O.D. Experiments: How Science is Discovering God in Everything, Including Us.* Atria Books, 2006

Skafte, Dianne, Ph.D. *Listening to the Oracle: The Ancient Art of Finding Guidance in the Signs and Symbols All Around Us.* HarperSanFrancisco, 1997

Smith, Penelope. *Animal Talk: Interspecies Telepathic Communication.* Beyond Words Publishing, Inc., 1999; original edition published by Pegasus Publications, 1982

Temple, Robert. *Oracles of the Dead: Ancient Techniques for Predicting the Future.* Destiny Books, 2005; originally published as *Netherworld: Discovering the Oracle of the Dead and Ancient Techniques of Foretelling the Future.* Century, 2002

Upczak, Patricia Rose. *Synchronicity, Signs & Symbols.* Synchronicity Publishing, 2001

Wood, Michael. *The Road to Delphi: The Life and Afterlife of Oracles.* Farrar, Straus and Giroux, 2003

ABOUT THE AUTHOR

Colette Baron-Reid, the author of *Remembering the Future,* is a popular spiritual intuitive, seminar leader, radio personality, motivational speaker, and musical recording artist on the EMI music label (with a top-selling meditation CD, *Journey Through the Chakras*). She has shared the stage with authors Sylvia Browne, John Holland, Caroline Myss, and many others. She currently lives in Sedona, Arizona; and Toronto, Canada, with her husband and their two furry children.

Website: **www.colettebaronreid.com**

NOTES

NOTES

NOTES

NOTES

NOTES

NOTES

NOTES

NOTES

NOTES

NOTES

We hope you enjoyed this Hay House book. If you'd like to receive a free catalog featuring additional Hay House books and products, or if you'd like information about the Hay Foundation, please contact:

Hay House, Inc.
P.O. Box 5100
Carlsbad, CA 92018-5100

(760) 431-7695 or (800) 654-5126
(760) 431-6948 (fax) or (800) 650-5115 (fax)
www.hayhouse.com® • www.hayfoundation.org

Published and distributed in Australia by: Hay House Australia Pty. Ltd., 18/36 Ralph St., Alexandria NSW 2015 • *Phone:* 612-9669-4299 *Fax:* 612-9669-4144 • www.hayhouse.com.au

Published and distributed in the United Kingdom by: Hay House UK, Ltd., 292B Kensal Rd., London W10 5BE • *Phone:* 44-20-8962-1230 *Fax:* 44-20-8962-1239 • www.hayhouse.co.uk

Published and distributed in the Republic of South Africa by: Hay House SA (Pty), Ltd., P.O. Box 990, Witkoppen 2068 • *Phone/Fax:* 27-11-467-8904 orders@psdprom.co.za • www.hayhouse.co.za

Published in India by: Hay House Publishers India, Muskaan Complex, Plot No. 3, B-2, Vasant Kunj, New Delhi 110 070 • *Phone:* 91-11-4176-1620 *Fax:* 91-11-4176-1630 • www.hayhouse.co.in

Distributed in Canada by: Raincoast, 9050 Shaughnessy St., Vancouver, B.C. V6P 6E5 • *Phone:* (604) 323-7100 • *Fax:* (604) 323-2600 • www.raincoast.com

Tune in to HayHouseRadio.com® for the best in inspirational talk radio featuring top Hay House authors! And, sign up via the Hay House USA Website to receive the Hay House online newsletter and stay informed about what's going on with your favorite authors. You'll receive bimonthly announcements about Discounts and Offers, Special Events, Product Highlights, Free Excerpts, Giveaways, and more! www.hayhouse.com®